Jimmy, Me & Autism

By

Sarah Pounder

Text copyright © to Sarah Pounder 2014

This book is sold under the condition that it shall not be lent, re-sold or hired out without the authors' prior consent.

Disclaimer

I have tried to recreate events, locales and conversations from my memories of them. In order to maintain their anonymity, in some instances I have changed the names of individuals and places. I may have changed some identifying characteristics and details such as physical properties, occupations and places of residence.

This book is not intended as a substitute for the medical advice of physicians. The reader should regularly consult a physician in matters relating to his/her health and particularly with respect to any symptoms that may require diagnosis or medical attention.

Acknowledgements

I would like to thank Dale for being the fantastic partner and father he is. He has been such a positive influence in my life. He has kept me level even when I have been at my lowest. Thank you for your strength and support. Also thank you to my three beautiful little boys, James, Adam and Joel, I love you all don't ever stop being you, your all perfect just the way you are.

I want to thank Bob Pounder for being the best dad a daughter could wish for. Dad, you have always been there to support and advise me when things have been tough, and the boys love the time they spend with you.

I wish to thank Dale's parents, June and Eddie Sheerin, for being lovely grandparents and for always being there when we need you.

Faye MacPherson and Claire Flowers, thank you for your continued support of ABA therapy for James and for being there for us.

A massive thank you to Ian McGrath, founder of the Hearts and Minds Challenge, and to Louise Gorman for helping us get James the educational provision he deserves. You have made a huge difference to our lives.

Thank you to cover designer Moll French, editor Joy Tibbs and advisor Peter Skillen for your continued help and support. I am eternally grateful.

A big thank you to anyone else I may have missed.

Foreword

When Sarah first contacted me around two years ago to congratulate me on writing my first book, she mentioned that she was also interested in writing a book. I asked her what she was planning to write about, and she told me all about her son Jimmy, who has severe autism.

I told Sarah that anyone can write a book. All you have to do is have great patience and perseverance, and make sure you finish what you start. Sarah told me this was the problem: she didn't know where to start. I simply said: "At the beginning."

I am often asked to advise people on how they can change their own lives as I did. I always recommend books people should read to kick-start their aspirations. This book you are about to read is one such book. It is the testament of a mother's love for her son and her determination to ensure that her son is able to live the best life possible.

This book is the result of Sarah's hard work, patience and tenacity; something she has in droves. You did it Sarah, and this book will be a shining example of hard work, dedication and determination to all.

Peter Skillen, BSc

Author of _The Twelve Step Warrior_, _Life is Good_ and _The Process_

Introduction

I want to introduce myself before you read my book. My name is Sarah and I'm thirty-four years old. I live with my partner Dale, who I have been with for twelve years, and we have three beautiful boys: James, who is eleven; Adam, who is nine; and Joel, who is four. I refer to Jimmy as James throughout the book as Jimmy is our nickname for him.

James is severely autistic. He also has attention deficit hyperactivity disorder (ADHD), sensory processing disorder (SPD) and profound learning difficulties. Adam has ADHD and oppositional defiant disorder (ODD). Joel seems fine; he has not displayed any conditions at all. It can be difficult for Joel because he copies a lot of his brothers' behaviours, but that is only to be expected among siblings. Despite their difficulties, all three boys are lovely, caring and very thoughtful. I love all three very much.

The story I'm about to tell you focuses on James and the problems we have faced as parents raising a child who is severely affected by autism. I have tried to describe honestly, and in detail, how difficult James' behaviour can be and the situations we have been in, especially for those who do not have an autistic child.

James was born on November 15, 2003. He was absolutely beautiful and Dale and I were so pleased with him. All I ever spoke about was James this and James that; he was so perfect.

I knew before everyone else that James was autistic, but I found the diagnosis very difficult to accept. The health visitor told me it can be like a mourning process for people, and sometimes it can take years to accept. I was told that my child was autistic and I was left to deal with it. No one could tell me what would happen, whether or not he would improve or what he would be like when he is older.

James' diagnosis has taken me a long time to get my head around and although I love my son with all my heart, I hated the autism. Some people may accept autism with open arms and say, '*It's part of my child and I love him for who he is*'. Well, I love my child, but I don't love autism. To me, I see it as a condition that truly disables my child. I see how debilitating it is and how much he struggles with life.

You would think that there are therapies out there that can provide coping strategies for autism, and there are. What you don't realise is that if you're not absolutely loaded they will be way beyond your reach, and to even get a sniff of them your local education authority (LEA) will make you fight tooth and nail for them.

The truly annoying thing for me is that, because James was born with autism and he is profoundly affected by this condition, the LEA wants to just bung James into a special educational needs (SEN) school – a one-size-fits-all education system – which, in our experience, does not work. It does not educate children like James; it simply means they are cared for within a school environment.

I can't help but feel that if James' condition had been the result of a serious accident the appropriate therapies and support would have been immediately available. It just doesn't seem fair that the decision-makers and the people in power haven't caught up with the realities of autism. These children should receive the equality they deserve to reach their full potential. Ignoring the needs of children like these will only serve to disadvantage them further.

As a parent, it feels empowering when your child receives the correct help and you can see the results. It gives you real hope for the future. Without this, the future would otherwise be bleak and eventually your child would become too big for you to handle. Then it is only a matter of time before you have to put your child into residential care.

This is a heartbreaking outcome, and far too much time is lost when early intervention and correct therapies is the key to success. This is why I'm writing this book; it's an honest view of what has happened to our family. I just hope that it touches and helps someone out there. I also hope someone in authority takes notice and tries to change things.

I have cried so much about James out of fear for his future and the frustration of not being able to access the correct help – which is available if you can get your hands on it – as well as the annoying experience of constantly being judged as a parent by professionals and the general public.

I am fed up with feeling like I need to put a T-shirt on my child that labels him as autistic because people are so unaware of autism. This is despite the fact that autism affects 700,000 people in the UK and touches the lives of 2.7 million people every day in the form of the friends and family members of those who are diagnosed with autism (figures from **autism.org.uk**).

I want to see better awareness of autism and I want children like James to be able to access proven early intervention therapies. I know that Applied Behaviour Analysis (ABA) does not suit every child, because each child is different, but I know that it works well for James. These children should be given tailor-made education programmes that mean something, and the progress should be quick and apparent for all to see. If the progress is not significant and visible, the child needs something different.

Parents should not be made to pay tens of thousands of pounds in court as we have just fighting to get the right type of education for our kids. The whole system seems corrupt to me. We have no rights. The government likes us to pretend we live in a democratic society, but unfortunately when we take the wrapping off it's just a well-dressed dictatorship in which uncaring professionals with no first-hand experience of raising a child with special educational needs push you around, telling you how it's going to be.

I will never stop fighting for my children; not until I take my last breath. They mean the world to me and whatever they need to get through life I will pursue until the very end. Never underestimate the fight within the parent of a special needs child.

CHAPTER ONE

My son James (Jimmy) was diagnosed with autistic spectrum disorder (ASD) at the age of three. He started to go through the assessment process when he was around eighteen months of age.

People always ask me when I first noticed James' autism and how I knew something was wrong. I noticed when he was around fifteen months old. I would walk into our living room and he would be sitting on the windowsill. I would tell him to get down and he did, and then I would look around and he would be sitting there on the windowsill again!

You may be thinking: *What's the big deal about him sitting on the windowsill?* Well, at the time the windows in our house were not double-glazed. They were in a state of disrepair and were thin, like picture glass. I was scared that he would fall through them, so I was constantly telling him to get down. This would go on all day, every day.

His repetitive behaviour was driving me crazy. He

just wouldn't do as he was told. This repetitive behaviour didn't just manifest itself on the windowsill. Another trait was his love for opening and shutting doors: open, shut, open, shut, the door would go. The fear of him trapping those little fingers in the door would cause me more anxiety; he didn't seem to understand the danger. He trapped his fingers a few times, yet never seemed to grow tired of opening and shutting the doors. Seeing that door opening and shutting, I can tell you, it drove me nuts. Even as I type I can feel the frustration.

Toy cars and toy kitchens were also subjected to this opening and shutting 'door obsession'. I didn't really mind this as much with toys because his couldn't cause any real harm to himself. It just left me scratching my head thinking: *Why is he not playing with this car properly?*

This was really just a passing thought. I was twenty-three when I had James and he was my first child. I wasn't used to children, so I didn't really know what was age-appropriate and what wasn't. I had nothing to compare him to; I just knew something wasn't right.

And there were other things that I had started to notice. When my partner Dale cut his toast in half, James would stand at the baby gate screaming. It took us a while to realise what the problem was, but then it dawned on us. He didn't like the change. Changing it from a whole piece of toast into half and then into quarters caused him to have a huge meltdown.

It was the same with bananas. If either of us peeled a banana, this was another thing that sparked off a massive temper tantrum. Again, change seemed to spark him off. Going from a banana with skin on it to seeing it peeled caused a problem.

The problem with upsetting James by doing these things, without realising it, was that it affected his mood all day. The tantrums weren't just little outbursts. He would become hysterical and it would take hours for him to calm down. Feeding times were a nightmare as soon as he went on to puréed foods. He would gag on certain foods and start to cry. Again, I never put two and two together.

The annoying thing is, it didn't matter whether it

was jarred food or homemade food. Our health visitors were always going on about making our own puréed food for babies because it had less salt and water in and was more nutritional. But I remember spending hours making batches of homemade baby food from a recipe book, only for James to scream and refuse to eat what I had made him.

To be honest, I think health visitors are absolutely right; I would only use pre-made baby food as a last resort. When you make your own food you know exactly what goes into it. Once you get your head around it and buy yourself a hand blender, it's easy.

***

When I was pregnant with my second child, Adam, I phoned the health visitor to discuss James' difficult behaviour. She asked me to come into the clinic with James for a chat. I remember telling her about my concerns. We must have been chatting for around an hour and I was explaining how difficult James was and the amount of stress he was causing me. I found him hard to deal with and his behaviour was irritating.

After observing James for an hour, she commented on how nicely he had sat and played while we chatted. Bear in mind that he had sat playing with a plastic kitchen for the whole hour, just opening and shutting the door. She sent me away with an NSPCC leaflet, which had snippets of information about dealing with toddlers. This provided illustrated features on preventing child abuse and revealed how smacking and shouting at your child was the wrong way to discipline him or her.

When I look back now, I knew it wasn't normal behaviour to be so obsessed with just one part of a toy. However, like a lot of other people I had heard of autism but knew nothing about it. I had never in my life come into contact with anyone who was autistic.

I find that most people are clueless about the symptoms of autism, and that most children do not get a diagnosis until they're older because parents, family members and even professionals think they will grow out of certain behaviours, especially if they are only slightly affected by the condition.

Even with James' severity level, family members would say, 'He's young; he'll grow out of it.' This didn't really help. Something wasn't right but I couldn't put my finger on it, mainly due to my lack of experience. I did shout at James a lot because of his temper tantrums, repetitive behaviour, not following instruction, and his total and utter defiance when it came to doing as he was told.

He continued to do annoying things, even if we sat down just for a few minutes. And the things he did couldn't be ignored, like trying to stick his fingers into the video player and plug sockets. You name it; if there was anything inappropriate and dangerous in sight he would play with it. In fact, he seemed to do it even more when we sat down.

Now I know you're probably thinking: *Duh! Has this parent never heard of plug socket protectors and a video lock?* Well, yes I have, and we had everything in place. But James being James, he worked them all out. He even worked out how to open the baby gate. Most adults cannot work this out. We used to say that he should have had a job testing children's safety gear out. It was literally nonstop.

It was strange, in a way. I can't say he carried on doing those things because he didn't understand, as sometimes he would do as he was told when we asked him to and other times we had to really shout to get his attention. He would stop the undesirable behaviour, but then within the space of a few minutes he would be back doing it all over again. Another thing he did while we were out and about was bolt off and eat things off the floor. To be honest, he drove me nuts. Most days I felt like screaming into a pillow in sheer frustration!

***

Another little problem Dale and I faced was James sleeping pattern. James slept through from six weeks old, which was brilliant. No one could believe it; he was such an easy baby. As James started to get older and his turbulent behaviour began, his sleeping pattern was affected. He went from being a contented baby who slept through to waking up in the middle of the night and screaming the house down.

I spoke to my auntie on the phone one day and told her about James waking up in the middle of the night. I told her it was starting to become a real problem because he was doing it every night. She told me that when her daughter was a baby she used controlled crying. She explained that when a child starts to cry in the night the parent walks into the child's room, doesn't speak or give any eye contact, lies the child back down so he or she is settled and walks back out of the room. When the child starts to cry again, the parent times it for two minutes and then repeats the process as many times as are necessary until the crying stops.

The parent is supposed to increase the number of minutes each time, but we just timed James for two minutes. We did this because we thought that if we left him any longer he would get into a real state and then it would be harder to settle him down. This sleep programme took us two weeks to master and, as it turned out, it was one of the best things we ever did.

Don't get me wrong, it was really hard and most parents would have just taken the child into bed with them, thinking that this is the easier option. Well, it isn't. Having a child sleeping in the same bed with you is not easier. They start off in their bed and then wake you up in the middle of the night to get in your bed, so you're still getting broken sleep.

I had James all day while Dale was at work. When he came home I would be going on and on about James being a pain in the neck. Dale would say: "What's up with you? That's what kids do! Why are you always moaning? I don't hear other mothers moaning about their kids like you do."

I would whinge to Dale's parents, to my dad and to anyone else that would listen. If something's not right, you will know about it with me! Rightly so in this case, because something wasn't right, although autism had never entered my head at this point.

***

I was heavily pregnant with Adam by this time and we had decided to put James into a private day nursery one day a week to soothe my moaning and to give me a break. This child was a handful. However, the morning he started nursery was the morning I went into labour, so I didn't even get to enjoy my first child-free day. Never mind!

I was in labour for three hours and I delivered Adam with just gas and air. Everything went smoothly apart from feeling as though I had done about ten rounds with Mike Tyson. Adam had really dark brown hair, which was a bit of a shock because James had been so blond when he was born, Dale's hair is still blond and I'm a dark blonde. I remember Dale looking at him, weighing him up, and me saying to him, "He's yours, you know. Don't worry; he's not the milkman's."

It's the best feeling in the world when you have a baby. It's like the best dream ever, only it's not a dream. You're wide awake and it's real. It just feels so surreal and so exciting. You can't sleep because you constantly want to stare at this little baby; your creation. To take in those little pink fingers and toes, the little noises they make and that lovely baby smell. That smell you stop being able to smell because you get used to it, but friends can still smell when they hold him close, as they're not as well acquainted with this tiny baby as you are.

***

I was transferred to the maternity ward shortly after Adam's birth. What an absolute nightmare, it was bedlam. It was like a children's day care centre with everyone's children just running around. The last thing you need when you've just given birth is to be stuck in a hospital ward with kids running round your bed. I heard one man ask if he could leave his kids on the ward for the day and the midwives reply was, "No! This is a maternity ward, not a nursery."

Luckily, Dale's mum June knew the midwife. She complained to her about some of the visitors and their out-of-control children. I was moved to my own room, which had a television. Adam and I had to stay in hospital for a few days because he needed a course of antibiotics. I have to say, being away from James was like heaven. What a break! And that's bad when you find yourself saying that a stay in hospital was a break.

It was Dale's turn to have a taste of James' behaviour. I'm not saying Dale had never had

James, because he did, but Dale worked full time, so I was the one who looked after and cared for him the most. I was his mum and that's what mums do, isn't it? Especially when you're a full-time mummy.

Dale came in with James during visiting hours. We introduced James to his new brother and there was no response, no interest, nothing! It was as though Adam didn't exist; as though he were an object rather than a person. James was running around the small side room we were in and it wasn't long before he noticed the open door and decided to run off down the corridor. So off down the corridor he ran.

Dale went after him, picked him up and brought him back to the room. James tried to get out and run off a few times. He was starting to get very agitated as he was being prevented from bolting. In the end we had to shut the door. As you can imagine, this did not go down well at all. There were two reasons for this: the first was that we were preventing him from doing what he wanted to do; and the second was that he hated doors being shut with a real passion.

He started to throw a massive tantrum. Dale and I found it hard to have a conversation because of James' escalating behaviour and we weren't really enjoying the hospital visit. Shortly after this, Dale took James home. He had decided to come back later and asked his mum to babysit James as it would have been his bedtime anyway. That way Dale and I could spend some time enjoying Adam.

When Dale arrived back at the hospital he told me how difficult James had been. I couldn't hold my sarcasm back any longer. I had to repeat one of the many things he had said to me in the past, when I was up to my neck in it with James' difficult behaviour.

"Take a deep breath and count to ten," I said. "Try not to shout." I just couldn't resist.

He gave me this knowing look that said: *I see where you're coming from now. It isn't as easy as I thought*. Dale having James for four days was exactly what he needed to give him an idea about how much of a handful this child really was.

***

The day had come to take Adam home. Dale came to pick me up from the hospital and my dad was looking after James at our house. It was tea time and my dad spent ages making James' tea as he knew how fussy James was about food. He had made him chicken and fried rice. Would James eat it? Not a chance. My dad was a little agitated, to say the least, because he had put a lot of effort into making James' tea, not to mention having looked after him for a few hours, which was, in itself, a major task.

James was always up to mischief from a young age and would always find something inappropriate or dangerous to play with. Anyone who looked after James had to have eyes in their bottom. If we left anything out that could pose some kind of risk to him he would notice it straightaway.

Obviously, no one is superhuman and human error is part of human nature, but you couldn't afford to make mistakes when James was around. It was like he knew what would cause total and utter bedlam. If you left the room it would have to be double-checked first to ensure that nothing untoward was left out.

My first encounter of this kind occurred when he realised he could reach the fish food. I had left the room and when I came back in there was fish food everywhere. He had been eating it. I had to phone NHS Direct, who told me not to worry as it was a vegetarian product.

This type of drama was just the tip of the iceberg. He would make a beeline for cleaning sprays, salt pots, glasses of wine; anything he shouldn't have. Occasionally these things would be left out, but most of the time they were placed out of reach and he would climb or drag a chair over to seek out the inappropriate item.

So this was what my dad had to deal with for the few hours we were at the hospital preparing to bring Adam home. Once everyone was settled after tea, I sat on the couch with Adam and tried to introduce him to his older brother. Once again, there was no interest there at all; it was as though Adam didn't exist.

I really couldn't get my head around James' apathetic behaviour towards Adam. I remember sitting on the couch holding Adam in my arms and feeling an overwhelming sense of guilt for bringing this new baby home. James shunning Adam felt like some sort of punishment, as though I had betrayed him somehow. This feeling didn't last very long. I suppose it was just a reaction to James' aloofness.

***

James had only been at the private day nursery for a couple of weeks when Helen, the nursery owner, approached me when I came to pick him up.

She said: "Do you mind if I have a quick word with you? It's about James. We have some concerns regarding his behaviour."

I thought, *Oh shit, what's all this about, then?* I couldn't for the life of me think why she was concerned. I found James' behaviour difficult, but I thought this was just me being soft.

Helen told me that one of her staff had reported an observation to her. "Sarah, we just wondered whether you have ever had any concerns about James' hearing," she said. "One of the girls, Kirsty, is concerned about James. He doesn't appear to be responding to his name."

I said: "I have thought that myself on a few occasions, to be honest, but when I've rustled something like a crisp packet, it has always got his attention straightaway."

Helen suggested that James might be suffering from a condition called glue ear and that it would be a good idea to mention it either to the doctor or a health visitor. She said this could be why James' hearing was so inconsistent.

As Adam was a newborn, the health visitor was coming around to the house frequently to perform newborn health checks. I decided to mention mine and the nursery's concerns about James during the next visit. The health visitor suggested that James should have a hearing test and said she would sort out a referral.

James was sitting at the dining room table playing with chunky crayons. She commented on how he was lining them up perfectly and that for a child of his age the crayons should at least have looked used. She also mentioned her concern over his intense concentration as he played with the door on his toy car. Open, shut, open, shut, over and over again, never growing bored. He just seemed to enjoy the mechanics of seeing it open and close.

She asked me all sorts of questions about his playing skills. She also commented on the fact that he wasn't really aware of, or interested in, strangers. Her presence in the house didn't bother him at all. It was as though she was part of the furniture; he didn't bat an eyelid.

The wording autism was mentioned a few times, and naturally when she left I googled it. Well, what's a parent to do? The whole thing started to come together piece by piece. I had known up to this point that something wasn't right, but autism? I had heard of it, but only because of *Rain Man*, a film that starred Dustin Hoffman as an autistic savant.

I didn't have a clue about autism; I knew nothing about its characteristics. The more I read, the more it clicked into place. Everything about it fitted with James. When Dale arrived home from work, I told him about my meeting with the health visitor and that she was making a referral for James' hearing to be tested. I also told him that she had mentioned autism a few times.

I told Dale I had looked into autism on the internet myself, but he wouldn't entertain the idea at all. It was as though he only heard the bits he could cope with, and when I mentioned autism he just shut me off completely. There was an immediate and instinctive denial there. It was like trying to talk to someone through glass. I was presenting my case and it wasn't taken into consideration; as though he hadn't even heard the words.

"He's only two," said Dale. "Stop being harsh. He'll grow out of it, and he'll catch up." He told me I was being really unfair.

***

The appointment for James' hearing test finally came through from the hospital. He was a real handful in the waiting room; running around and messing with things he shouldn't have been playing with. He never sat still, which meant I couldn't sit still either, for fear of his inappropriate behaviour.

If there were other children around whom we didn't know, he wouldn't think twice about going over to them and taking whatever they had from them. Standing in the waiting room hovering over James, on tenterhooks with the dread of what he might do next, James' name was called.

James ran straight into the treatment room without any hesitation at all. He gave the staff in that room no acknowledgement whatsoever. He was just drawn to the toys on the floor. The medical staff tried to introduce themselves to him, but he simply ignored them. The thing is it wasn't just James' difficult behaviour that was the problem. This child couldn't speak a word or follow basic instructions. He was nearly two and he had no language at all.

The only communication James had was his ability to display two types of emotion: happy or sad. If he was happy he would laugh and if he was sad he would cry. But he couldn't express himself; he just didn't have the language to do so.

James just got on with what he wanted to do. On this occasion, it was playing with a little wooden boat with little wooden people in it. He loved it. He kept putting the pieces in and taking them back out again. I was bemused because it was the first time I had seen him play with an object that wasn't a door. I even asked the audiologist where it had come from so I could go out and buy him one. Unfortunately, she didn't know.

I could see how engrossed James was and I started to wonder how the audiologist would carry out the hearing test. She reassured me and said that they would be able to tell whether he had heard the sound as they were looking for facial reaction. She pointed out that they also tested different sound frequencies to check whether there were any underlying problems preventing him from hearing certain sound waves.

At the end of James' examination she concluded that he did not have glue ear and that there was nothing wrong with James' hearing. She said she wanted to see him in a few months' time to review him, but other than that they were happy with the outcome of his hearing test and a report would be sent to our doctor's surgery.

I walked James back up to my dad's house, which was a ten-minute walk from the hospital. My dad had been looking after Adam so that I didn't have to take him to the appointment as well.

I recall thinking to myself, *Shit, shit, shit. This is not good. This is not good at all. If it's not a hearing problem, it is definitely autism.*

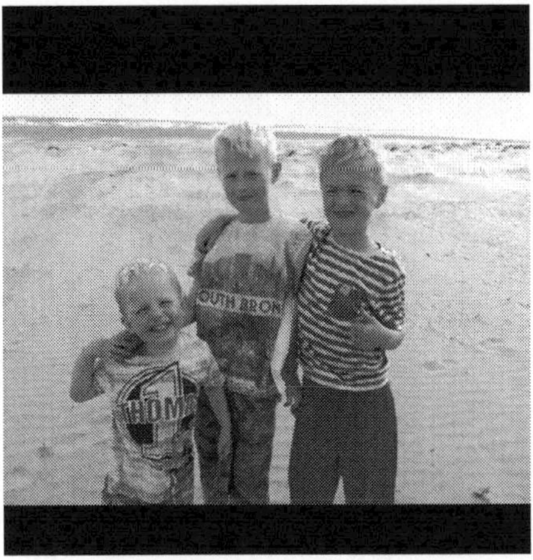

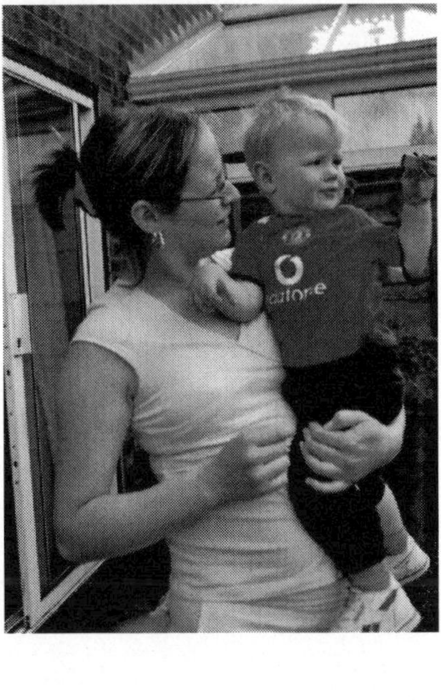

CHAPTER TWO

James was still attending the private day care nursery, despite the problems he had had. Members of staff at the nursery were aware that James' hearing was not an influencing factor in terms of his unruly nature, but looking back they knew that anyway. Most children who are slightly affected by autism slip through the net, but not James. There was no denying the fact that his behaviour was more than just a blip.

James was placed on a waiting list to be seen by a multi-agency team at the child development unit. I had to wait months and months for his appointment to come through. During this long wait I felt like ripping my hair out in desperation. It was a combination of the stress, the not knowing and the fact that people didn't believe me, including family members.

Sometimes you're made to feel like it's not the child that has the problem, but you. I was made to feel like I had Munchausen syndrome because other people were determined to bury their heads in the sand, simply because they were in denial.

I got to the point where I was so stressed I would phone the child development unit to chase up the appointment and see if we could have it sooner. I often cried down the phone because I was so desperate for help. Not only was I finding it difficult to manage James' behaviour, I was being made to feel as though I had a mental health problem because other people simply couldn't face the facts.

I would pick James up from nursery each day. He was only doing half a day to begin with, and I used this time to do research. The more I delved, the more information I got. I was grateful for the information, because the more information I got the more I understood about autism. How can you help your child if you don't know what you're dealing with?

I would also get the low-down on what he had been up to in the day from the nursery staff. I'm not being flippant here, as the nursery staff simply expressed their concerns about James' abnormal activity. I would hear stories about him climbing onto the water pool table rather than just standing with the rest of the children, who only put their hands in it. They would tell me that they had caught him eating PVA glue, glitter, sand and paint.

The next nightmare we had was James stuffing things up his nose, such as paper and crayons. They went up a treat. Then he would get stressed because he couldn't get them out and I would hear him crying and sniffing, as well as frantically rubbing his nose; more because it was uncomfortable than out of panic.

Other issues were becoming more and more apparent, and little things were becoming more of a problem every day. It was very, very stressful to say the least. Going to the local mums and tots group had to stop. When Adam was a newborn I took him and James one Monday morning to show Adam off. I hadn't been there long before Adam was due his feed. I left James sitting at a table with the other children, who were cutting and sticking pieces of paper.

I asked some of the other parents if they would

watch James as I had to go and get Adam's bottle warmed. The kitchen was run by old ladies who volunteered to make all the snacks for the children.

While I was waiting for the bottle to warm, one of the parents brought James back to me. She said: "I've had to bring him back, Sarah, I don't know what to do with him! He's eating all the PVA glue."

So there I was standing at the kitchen serving hatch with Adam in my arms and a very impulsive James running around. There were tables laid out near the kitchen with snacks on them ready to be served to the children at the playgroup. James spotted the snacks straight away and began stuffing the food into his mouth. The next thing I knew, all the old ladies started telling him off and I couldn't do anything about it with my arms full. James was running around as though he had never been fed.

This was the last time we went to mums and tots. Never again! It was far too stressful and James looked like a wild animal who didn't understand basic rules and boundaries. I couldn't bear to take him back to that playgroup, especially as I wasn't able to explain what the issue was. It made me feel terrible having people sitting there staring and judging.

***

Even before Adam was born, people I knew would come over to James in the street to have a chat and they would try to engage with him. There was no attempt to communicate, no eye contact or recognition from James; there was nothing. He would just look through people as though they weren't there. He went from being a baby who laughed and interacted to a child who was really withdrawn, like someone had stolen his fun personality during the night.

I remember having this horrible uneasy feeling all the time because I couldn't explain the issue to people. I started to get paranoid, subconsciously thinking about what other people might be thinking about James' vacant persona. I was thinking all kinds of crazy things like, *Oh my God, people are going to think he's some sort of abused child or something?* and *Why does this child seem like such an unhappy little boy?*

It was as though he had an air of sadness around him and, because I could see it, it also made me feel very sad inside. You can see why professionals blamed autism on parenting at one time. Back in the day I would have been labelled as a 'refrigerator mother': a theory that claimed the child wasn't receiving enough maternal love.

This was far from true. James was well loved and was never short of cuddles and kisses. He was all I talked about, even on a night out. One thing I was guilty of before I had children was saying: "I'm not hanging around with such and such a body, she's a baby bore." And here I was being guilty of it myself. I was the queen of baby bores and I cherished him so much. He was all I ever talked about.

***

My close friend Debbie had noticed that the behaviours James was displaying were odd. Her daughter is two months older than James, so she could quite easily compare differences, and she also had an older child. Before I had Adam she looked after James for half a day while Dale and I attended a hospital appointment for my twenty-week scan. Even to this day she talks about how he sat on the floor spinning a plastic milk carton around and around.

It was so repetitive that her daughter Grace took the carton from him and he went berserk. Debbie took the carton away from Grace and threw it back to James in a panic. She said she had never seen anyone so focused on spinning a milk carton before. She spoke to her partner Lee that night about her concerns over James' behaviour: the spinning of the carton, his lack of social responses and the absence of speech.

I recall having conversations with Debbie about my concerns, but this was after the nursery had brought the problems to my attention. Debbie is a very good friend of mine and she was never intrusive with her opinions about James, although she did mention the carton spinning. I understand that it was never her place to say her piece and I respect that, and she has always has been a good, supportive friend. She says now that she had a friend whose son had Asperger's and the traits James was presenting were similar to those her friend's son had.

"How could I tell you there was something wrong with your firstborn child?" she asked afterwards. "I just couldn't do it to you. I also had self-doubt. I thought I might have been wrong as I was no expert."

***

The time came when Adam was at the stage of sitting up and the next problem I had was James running over and pushing him over. This was absolutely awful. It was also very dangerous because we didn't have carpet. We had laminate flooring, so the landing wasn't at all soft. It was a nightmare. It was as though James had found a new obsession.

I couldn't get my head around this malicious behaviour. The way I tried to discipline James was to tell him off and send him straight to his room.

Like any of James' obsessions it was repetitive and would happen very regularly throughout the day. James was very impulsive, so we couldn't tell when he was about to do it. I would just hear a thud followed by a cry.

It was very hard to keep James and Adam separate in our house because we had the tiniest kitchen ever and the living room was a through room. I did my very best to keep them apart. If I needed the toilet it meant one of them had to come with me. I would never go upstairs and leave Adam alone with James.

Another problem I had with sending James to his room as a punishment was that he punished me back. The beautiful bedroom we had made him was being dissembled piece by piece. He would wee all over the carpet, bed or furniture, or he would smear poo into the carpet and walls. I was up to boiling point with him. I felt like handing him over to someone or walking out at times.

One afternoon I was back on the phone chasing up James' appointment. I was angry and frustrated as he had just pushed Adam over again and I felt as though I couldn't take it any longer. I had put James upstairs in his bedroom as a punishment, and as I was on the phone crying in desperation about his behaviour I heard this almighty crash coming from upstairs. Still with the phone in my hand I went running upstairs to find that James had ripped one of his wardrobe doors off. I explained to the woman on the phone what he had just done. But although she sympathised with me it still didn't make a difference to the waiting list.

Both boys had beautifully decorated bedrooms. Each had plastered cream walls with an individual border around them. James had the bigger bedroom. In James' room the vents for the radiators had been ripped off and the curtains had been pulled down. The wardrobe had to have ties around the handles to stop him ripping the wardrobe doors off.

Toys would get launched around the room and often he used them to climb on, so the fewer toys he had in there the better. Too many things seemed to overload him and make his behaviour worse. He also ripped all the bedding of his bed and dragged the mattress off. It was like walking into complete chaos. On top of all the other irritating behaviours James displayed, he had no regard for the environment he lived in, or what was right and wrong. He had no empathy for anyone else's feelings either.

I got a knock at the door one night from a neighbour called John who lived in a house that was back to back with ours. Dale and I opened the front door and he said: "Did you know your son is walking up and down the windowsill?"

We told John that we knew James did this, that he did it every night and there was nothing we could do to stop him doing it unless we physically held him, and this wasn't an option.

He said: "I had to come round and tell you, because my sister fell through a window when we were kids. I see him doing it every night; it goes through me."

We reassured John, telling him not to worry and that we were aware that James was doing it. We were sure he couldn't come to any harm because his bedroom window was double-glazed by this point and we always made sure his windows were locked with a key if he was in there.

***

James' appointment eventually came through and he was offered an appointment at the child development unit for an assessment. I had to take him on my own as Dale wouldn't even engage in conversation with me about James having serious problems. Dale's family didn't agree with me either. They just saw James as a little boy who was slightly behind his peers and believed that he would catch up.

Dale and I had a huge row about James one night because I wanted to discuss the problems and to talk about the assessment. He went mad, telling me I was out of order. He was going ballistic, shouting at the top of his voice: "I don't want to talk about it and that's final! And I'm telling you now he's not going to that Cherry Tree School."

I couldn't get a word in and I couldn't reason with him. All I needed was his support. It turns out that the school James attended later on was for more severe pupils. The Cherry Tree School was a special needs school, but for those who are more severely affected went to Ravens Hill Primary School.

Dale's dad was also saying that we shouldn't be getting James labelled, which infuriated me even more. I thought, *Who are we not getting him labelled for? You! If this child needs a label to get the right help then that's what he needs. I'm struggling with bringing this child up. I'm worried to death as it is and all I'm getting is, "Don't get him labelled." Like I've got a choice anyway.*

It was so obvious there was something wrong with James. It wasn't like we could just brush it under the carpet and pretend the whole thing wasn't happening. That's the powerful thing about denial. If we pretend things aren't happening we think they will go away, but they don't. The problem gets bigger and bigger, and sooner or later we have to face facts.

If I can give anyone a piece of really good advice, it is to remember this: if you have any suspicions or a gut feeling that your child is on the autistic spectrum, react now. The longer you leave a child with autism, the longer it takes to reach them. Early intervention is the key, but it has to be the correct form of intervention (more on this later).

***

James' appointment at the child development unit meant he would need to attend every day for a period of two weeks. James wasn't the only child being assessed; a few children were there. I didn't realise this at the time, but the reason they do this is to see how the children interact with each other. Children on the autistic spectrum have a lack of imaginative play and find it very difficult to interact with their peers.

James was assessed by a team of nine professionals. The team consisted of: a paediatric doctor, an occupational therapist (OT), a speech and language therapist (SALT), a clinical psychologist, a nursery nurse, a family support worker and an educational psychologist. The other two assessments were carried out by my dentist, based at the family practice, and the audiologist, based at the hospital. I had to attend every day with James and I also had to take Adam to the unit with us.

One of James' appointments was with the OT. Her input was that there was no squint detected and that James demonstrated the ability to use his eyes together as a pair. She also stated that it was not possible to test James' levels of vision due to his lack of interest in the test material. It was an absolute nightmare trying to get him to participate during that appointment. All he wanted to do was mess around with things a child shouldn't be messing with.

The next day Dale's sister Emma attended one of the appointments with me. It was an appointment with the paediatric doctor. On the way there Emma was trying to reassure me that everything was fine with James and that I had nothing to worry about. She said that her mum was scared and that was why my mother-in-law didn't want to get into conversation with me about James' assessments.

While I was being interviewed by the doctor about

James' health, all James wanted to do was play with the taps. He was switching the water on and off in the sink in the small side room. It was very distracting and I had to keep telling him to stop as his fascination with water often meant that he ended up soaked through and the room would have ended up flooded. The paediatric doctor wrote in her report that James' general health was good and an annual review was suggested.

James then saw a speech and language therapist. These professionals ask you all sorts of questions going back to pregnancy, birth and right up to date, so you can imagine how long the appointments took.

The speech therapist stated in her report that James had a severe social communication disorder. This was inhibiting both verbal and nonverbal areas of his communication development, which was affecting his ability to interact with other people. She stated that James appeared unaware of the social rules of communication and that he did not understand the need for eye contact. She pointed out that James also had great difficulty listening to, processing and understanding language, which was preventing him from communicating properly.

Another day, another appointment. James was seen by the clinical psychologist next and her observation was that James was a very active little boy. She said that James had the triad of impairments that are associated with the autistic spectrum. The triad of impairments affect: social communication, social imagination and social relationships. She said that our family would benefit if we attended a support group for autism and referred us to an early intervention team that had been set up to help with autism.

The other person who completed a report about James was the child development team's nursery nurse. She said James actively explored the playroom environment. However, she stated that his concentration was very fleeting and that it was very difficult to engage him in play. Making a connection with James had to be on his terms.

She went on to say that James' play was solitary, in keeping with a child much younger than his age, and that he was very limited in his choice of toys, which he mouthed (put them inside his mouth) before he began to play with them. She pointed out that James was unaware of children who were in close contact with him, so his social interaction was limited and he appeared to be in a world of his own.

Inappropriate play came up in the assessment when she observed James drinking water out of the bucket during water play and repeatedly casting sand on the floor. She also noticed that he occasionally sought out a familiar adult, and that he communicated by pulling the adult's hand towards a desired item. She noted that he cuddled up to adults to seek emotional support.

The report said that he could be insistent and would become frustrated and scream at a high pitch if his needs were not met immediately. It also explained that a lot of direction was needed during creative sessions and that his self-help skills were developing with guidance. At the end of the report it said that James was a lovely little boy and that I had been on hand throughout the assessment process to offer him lots of support and encouragement.

At the end of the two weeks, everyone had collected their evidence and it was put into one detailed report. Dale and I had to attend the meeting to find out the team's overall findings. Kirsty, James' nursery nurse from the private day care nursery, attended the meeting so that she could find out what was going on with James. She also put her concerns across.

James was not given a clear diagnosis of autism at this meeting because he was so young, even though the reports suggested that he was autistic. The head clinical psychologist, Lisa Wingler, who chaired the meeting, kept referring to James as having a severe social communication disorder.

This didn't really highlight the intensity of the problems James was experiencing. Instead they kind of glossed things over so as not to cause us any alarm. It left me feeling numb and confused about the whole situation. It was only as time went on and things started to unfold that I realised we were well and truly up shit creek and that this was only the tip of the iceberg.

***

Dale and I ended up having another meeting with Lisa Wingler at our home. Luckily for me, I have a partner who not only has a strong personality but sees things very much in black and white. There are no grey areas with Dale at all. Because of his previous job at the council he was used to being in a meeting environment, so he knew exactly how to put the pressure on.

He said: "You're telling me my son has a severe communication disorder! What exactly does this mean?"

Lisa answered: "James displays the triad of impairments that are associated with autistic spectrum disorder."

Dale replied: "What are we supposed to say when people ask us what's wrong with our son?"

Lisa said: "Tell them he has a severe communication disorder."

Dale then pointed out: "You've just said that he has the triad of impairments associated with autism! What are you saying? He's either autistic or he's not, which one is it?

"Okay, okay. If people ask, you might as well tell them he's autistic."

This was how James' autism was confirmed.

The diagnosis wasn't finalised for another year. They do this because small children can make rapid progress and they have to make sure the child isn't misdiagnosed. I had to attend yet another appointment so James could be assessed by a senior speech and language therapist.

The senior SALT carried out an assessment on him known as the Autism Diagnostic Observation Schedule (ADOS). This is a diagnostic tool used to identify the triad of impairment: social interaction, imaginative play and communication impairment.

For the first part of the examination he was assessed on communication and language score, which ranges from zero to twelve. Four and above signifies autism, and James scored eight. He was also assessed on reciprocal social interaction, with scores ranging from zero to fourteen. Anything above six indicates autism, and James scored thirteen. James was also examined for play behaviours. The report stated that there was no pretend or symbolic play during the session.

My child was three years and three months old when the assessment was carried out, and the report states that he was mouthing toys. A baby might be expected to mouth toys, but not a three-year-old. The report at the end said that James' scores indicated autistic spectrum disorder. He didn't really need the assessment. It was clear just by looking at the way he behaved in day-to-day life that he was badly affected by autism.

Maybe having read all of the above you think I'm being harsh and cold. This isn't my intention. I have written this account because it's all true. And for those of you who do not have a child with autism or have never come across autism in your life, I'm doing my best to describe how difficult it really is. I love James with all my heart, despite how difficult he is. Autism is not what I wanted for him, but that's who he is and I can tell you I've cried buckets over this because I have felt torn apart inside.

CHAPTER THREE

All the problems associated with James being in the bigger bedroom were starting to cause a lot of stress. I couldn't store his toys in there and there was the issue of him walking up and down the windowsill. In the end I thought life would be easier if the boys swapped rooms.

Even this wasn't straightforward as I had to convince Dale, and he took some convincing. Dale's argument was that the bigger room was James' and that it wasn't fair to change it; that doing so could cause childhood resentment. I wouldn't let up as it was me who cared for the boys the most. I had to have the house running smoothly and in a way that I could manage without all the added stress.

Dale eventually understood my reasons for wanting to swap the boys' rooms and agreed to do it. I needed his help as it wasn't just a straightforward swap. The window in the other bedroom wasn't 'James proof'. It was the original window, so there were no safety restrictors on it and it was a side opener.

I stayed at my dad's house with James and Adam while Dale fitted a new UPVC, double-glazed window in what was to become James' bedroom. It took the whole weekend to sort out. I found it difficult staying at my dad's house because James struggled to settle at bedtime in an unfamiliar setting.

On the Sunday night I brought James and Adam back home, feeling glad that the rooms had been swapped around to make life easier, but James had another little trick up his sleeve. The baby gate we used for his room was one he hadn't worked out how to open, but he wasn't overly impressed with his new room, so he worked out how to climb over it.

I needed a baby gate on his room to set the boundary that it was night time. It gave me some control, stopping him running all over the house and giving me peace of mind that he was safe. There's nothing worse than having someone sneaking around upstairs knowing that they're definitely up to no good.

I couldn't be doing with that, so I spoke to Elaine, my key worker from the children with disabilities team. Elaine organised for an OT to come round to the house to do an assessment on his bedroom. They agreed to send a joiner round to the house. He had made two large gates that were half the size of a standard door to prevent James from climbing over the top. One was for the kitchen door to stop him going into the kitchen and upstairs, and the other was to keep him in his bedroom. When the gates were put on I felt a huge sense of relief. I knew this would make life easier and give me one less thing to worry about.

Later that day, I got a phone call from the joiner. "Hiya love, it's Paul speaking. I think I've left my wood glue in the bedroom upstairs!"

I ran upstairs to check, and there it was on the bedroom carpet. I breathed a sigh of relief that it had not been touched. The reason it hadn't been touched was that the new gates had been fitted and

James had been in the front room all day. Thank God for that, because if he had seen it before I did it would have been a disaster. This is how easy it is to mess up where James is concerned. He would have had a field day with that glue, especially as he puts everything in his mouth.

***

James wasn't impressed at all by the new gates but he got used to the change just as he eventually got used to his new room. He had kicked off the first night in the new room, which caused a bit of friction between me and Dale.

"Sarah, I told you we shouldn't have swapped his room around," Dale said.

I raised my voice through panic and in order to make my case: "Look, Dale. He'll get used to it. I can't have him ruling the roost. Life's hard enough as it is."

Dale and I now have a very good understanding of how to deal with James. I know there will be some people out there who may disagree with our parenting, for example the parents who have strict timetables, always drive the same way to a place or have certain music on to avoid a huge meltdown because their child is autistic. Some will think we are wrong and harsh because of the anxiety we have caused our child.

Our theory is that we don't live in an autistic world; a perfect world in which everything goes the 'right' way. We live in an unpredictable world; a world that can change at the drop of hat. So we decided that James would have to learn to accept change. Life is all about change and I would rather he had a temper tantrum at a young age than end up getting my face kicked in when he's an adult because he has low tolerance levels when it comes to a change of plan.

By doing this he'll have a better understanding on a communication level and learning to tolerate change will provide James with self-regulation techniques and self-controlled behaviours from adolescence through to adulthood. We have had to bring James up in this way. He hasn't been the easiest child to bring up but we've had to persist with it, otherwise our lives would be unbearable.

Some things were unavoidable. If one of us got out of the car to go into a shop or petrol station, all hell would break loose. At times, life has been really unbearable for us. The pressure of getting out of that car and being stuck in a queue while some dithering tit who has all day to do what they're doing would really get my blood going because I knew I was going to get it in the neck when I got back in the car.

"God, where have you been? You've been ages and he's been going absolutely mental."

It was really annoying, especially seeing as it was something that was beyond my control. We were justified in getting angry being stuck in a car with a screaming James, with his white blond hair that seemed to look increasingly fibrotic the more he got into his tantrum.

This wouldn't just be a little cry or even a big

screaming session; he would become furiously violent. He would slouch down in his car seat, overextend his legs and begin kicking whoever was in the front of the car. Another thing he would do was headbang. This was done with force, to the point that the headrest had collapsed. He also used to bang his head against the glass windows. What do you do? Not live your life? Not go out anywhere? Become a prisoner to autism? No way. This sort of thing was going on all the time and was becoming worse the older he got.

***

Another problem I experienced was I couldn't toilet-train James and the nursery wouldn't do it, so there was no consistency between his time at nursery and his time at home. James also seemed to have a problem with his gut. He sometimes had bowel movements up to seven times a day, and it was like diarrhoea. This was a real hindrance. Not only was I changing nappies all day; I didn't have the support to even begin to get him out of them.

If you take into consideration the number of times

James opened his bowels in a day, I never seemed to be done cleaning faeces from the walls, carpets and furniture. He would do it in the morning when he had been sent upstairs for being naughty, and at bedtimes. It was apparent that he derived some enjoyment from pasting the walls, carpet and furniture with poo and then smearing it all over himself. What a wonderful time I had cleaning it up afterwards!

Whenever it happened I had a day from hell. I had to wash him down and put him in a different room while I set about cleaning his bedroom. I had mixed emotions: I was feeling absolutely furious, wanting to cry with the frustration and desperate to scream the house down for some kind of release. My chest would feel so tight and heavy. No matter how many times I took a deep breath to try to release this feeling of stress, it wouldn't budge. It normally took a full night's sleep or a couple glasses of wine to come down from that feeling.

Dale and I were finding James' difficult behaviour very hard work. There was no let-up. We had concerns that James had no speech, that his behaviour was out control and that he needed help to get on the right track. I had already taken numerous courses set up by the local education authority (LEA) at Ravens Top primary school. I took whatever was offered.

I got very excited about one of the courses and was chuffed to bits that James got it. It was a brief introduction to the way the picture exchange communication system (PECS) works.

A few children attended this appointment. It took two therapists to carry out the picture exchange procedure and I was amazed at what I saw. James was sitting at the table with one therapist sitting in front of him and the other sitting behind. The therapist at the front had a bowl of grapes and the one at the back had a small laminated card with a symbol on. This particular symbol had a picture of grapes on it.

The therapist in front had the grape in her hand where he could see it, and she held her hand out. He went to grab the grape, but the therapist sitting behind him quickly put the symbol in his hand so he could exchange it for the grape. It only took a few goes for him to grasp the concept. He did so very,

very quickly. I was amazed and felt high as a kite. This opened up a doorway to a whole new world. The possibilities were endless and this proved that my child had the potential to learn. Yippee! What a breakthrough!

***

The problem I found with the symbols was that they weren't very lifelike and he found it difficult to distinguish between the pictures. Back at home he was trying to give me any old symbol for an item of food. We used food items to make the picture exchanges because food is often a big motivator for children on the autistic spectrum.

We needed to help James distinguish between the different pictures, so Dale and I decided to use photographs instead. I ended up driving straight to the supermarket to pick up a laminator and laminating sheets, and then I went about taking photographs of James' favourite food items. Surprisingly enough, this worked an absolute treat. The photos were so lifelike to James that he picked it up brilliantly. We made sure we were strict about using the photos rather than having James stand at the kitchen door shouting "Arghh" and pointing.

We had a lot of laminated photographs stuck to the kitchen door with double-sided Velcro. This worked well, although sometimes James would take them off the door. Then when he made a request for something with his only form of communication – "Arghh" – we would say: "James, go and get your PECS!"

But then he couldn't find them and we would spend the next however long helping him look through the chaos of overturned toy boxes. This was the annoying thing with PECS. Even though it initially works it can be a long, slow process, which goes right through to sentence building. Nine years down the line we're still not at that level.

We had to use PECS consistently, in all environments. Even other people who had him in their care had to do the same thing, and that was easier said than done. When we went out anywhere we had to take a file out with us. There was even a PECS symbol with a red cross on it stuck to the light switch, which was meant to a deterrent telling him not to keep playing with the light switch. All he did was pull a chair up and rip the PECS symbol off before throwing it to the floor and carrying on with his light flicking.

We tried to focus a lot on James' speech, repeating words over and over again, but he had no language at all and the lack of eye contact didn't help. He couldn't even imitate speech or movement. He had stopped waving goodbye at ten months, and he couldn't even imitate that simple movement. How do you teach a child to speak when he is only interested in his own internal world? Trying to hold James' attention while mouthing the words was proving difficult, hence the problem he had discriminating between the different PECS symbols.

Dale and I really wanted to get James the right help and we saw straightaway that consistency was key. We knew he had the ability to learn, and even though I have said some negative things about PECS it did the job, and it certainly showed us that James has the ability to learn.

***

We were becoming more and more concerned about James' lack of progress and out-of-control behaviour. We felt it was absolutely paramount that our son got specialised help, and sooner rather than later if he was to stand any chance of living in the real world. We couldn't bear the temper tantrums, the poo smearing, the constant worry about his non-existent awareness of his own personal safety and the difficulties surrounding his communication skills.

We knew deep down that he had the capability to learn, but somehow he had to be taught these skills to reach the developmental milestones he needed to get on in life. While other children learn naturally, James somehow needed to be taught these skills, bit by bit. We so desperately wanted to reach him and unlock his potential.

We had come to the end of the road with the Private Day Nursery. There wasn't really anything more they could do to help us. James was also at the age when he needed potty training and the nursery wouldn't help us do this. As James had loose stools and needed very frequent nappy changes, they didn't really have the staff levels to cope.

It had also been mentioned in a previous meeting that James really needed one-to-one support, but the nursery owner couldn't afford or justify having a member of staff solely employed for James. This obviously wasn't the right setting for James. You cannot part potty train a child, especially if he or she is autistic. Life is confusing enough for autistic children as it is.

***

By this time, James had been assessed by Wayne Floods, an educational psychologist from our LEA. He was assessed at the Private Day Nursery. His report gave an overview of the delay in James' delay development compared with his peers. It said that, at three years and three months, James' speech was still at the babbling stage. Some use of words, such as "all gone" had been used, but this was inconsistent.

The speech and language stage he was at was typical of a child between the age of nine and twelve months. Again, Wayne Floods also picked up on observations that have previously been mentioned in earlier reports The report said that James would grab the hand of an adult to guide him or her towards a need or a want, and this was spot on. It noted that he would respond to his name but not to other words.

The report also stated that James had a variety of behavioural difficulties, which I knew about because I was experiencing them at home. It had been noted that James became physically aggressive towards other children, especially at the end of the day when he was tired, or when an adult or child entered or left the room. He also struggled to sit down during group times. His behaviour was affected by high noise levels and by the presence of a large number of other children.

It observed that at times he didn't appear to be aware of other children around him, although his tolerance at meal times and the length of time he was able to work alongside peers had improved. James was being removed by staff for one-to-one work when he became unsettled. It was recorded that James recognised familiar adults in photographs, but that he lost interest in toys that were shown to him and then put out of sight, and that he did not seek hidden items.

As the report unfolded, it summarised that James' receptive and expressive language was very low compared with other children of his age. His communication interactions were limited, and he was only proactive about engaging with other people to gain food or other desired items rather than to share experiences.

The recommendations given in the report were that James needed access to a teaching and learning approach that reflected the involvement of speech and language therapy along with routines that included visual prompts. He also needed to work with adults who were experienced in working with communication approaches such as PECS, and that he needed to be able to discriminate between symbols consistently.

It said that James would benefit from a high-ratio adult-to-child educational setting, as this would extend his engagement to activities. The report recommended a setting in which the number of other children around him was more controlled, with gradual exposure to busier environments.

We weighed up our situation with James and decided we didn't want to wait a minute longer. We wanted the help right away; we needed it right away. We were so anxious and James' behavioural outbursts weren't getting any easier to handle. The things that worked with normal children – including all the stuff you see on *Supernanny* – didn't work with James.

We felt helpless because there was nowhere to turn for specialist help for the problems we had with James. Programmes like *Supernanny* made us feel a bit left out because we didn't fit 'the norm'. Maybe it would be helpful to make television programmes for the autistic spectrum with an autism 'supernanny' who would go to the homes of special needs parents so that parents like us could see proven behavioural techniques and different hints and tips that deal with a range of issues across a wide-ranging spectrum. This could prove very beneficial, especially when people are going through the diagnosis process.

***

We phoned Wayne to arrange a meeting at our house about the possibility of James attending the local special needs school. We hoped the school would be specialised enough to deal with James.

There was quite a bit of debate about this because James wasn't due to start nursery until the September, but we knew of parents who had already had a child in the special educational needs nursery at the same age. We knew by the end of this meeting that everything was to do with cost. We stated our case and explained why we were desperate for the help. Wayne said that our case would have to be presented to a panel and that this would not take place for another two weeks.

The time came and I received a phone call saying that James had been accepted into the nursery. It was such a relief that James would start receiving some proper help and support. We believed the possibilities were endless. I thought with the nursery's specialism in autism that James would come on leaps and bounds with his speech and communication skills, that we could get him out of nappies and see him independently using the toilet. We felt the nursery would also help and support us in dealing with James' behaviour, since they were used to dealing with severely autistic children. They would have the experience to help us manage and cope while giving us some hope, right?

Up to this point we had felt as though we were looking into a dark tunnel with no light at the end of it. That feeling leads to sensations of helplessness and despair. Things feel stagnant and you feel like you're treading water with your head just about sticking out. I was feeling like there was nothing really out there to help us with that lack of hope. I needed inspiration and new ideas to help us cope with James.

I would be sitting downstairs when James went to bed. All would be well and quiet, so I would have time to think and step out of the situation. This meant that a really bad day got ten times worse when I was sitting there thinking about the day's events. I would beat myself up about everything I had said and handled badly that day.

I would feel so bad because I had shouted at James all day because there had been no let-up from him playing with dangerous items and recurring temper tantrums that could last for an hour or more. I would sit there thinking it all through, telling myself: "I will do better to tomorrow, I won't get stressed. I will keep my calm, I will do better."

Then I would go upstairs to peek through the door to check that he was safe, because with a child like James we soon came to realise that compulsive checking of his personal safety was absolutely vital. Then, just before I reached the door I would realise he wasn't tucked up in bed having run me ragged all day. No! I would hear him squealing with delight and the next sense to be called upon would be my sense of smell. There was that unforgettable smell you cannot dismiss: the smell of poo!

My stomach would drop to the pits of hell and I would get a horrible, sinking feeling accompanied by panic because I would realise that my poo day, if you'll excuse the pun, was not quite over. Then, when I opened the bedroom door, I would find a naked James smearing poo into the carpet. His body would be covered in it. It would all be in his nails, on his feet, face and torso. Then I would glance around at the rest of the room and it would be all over the walls.

Do the textbook professionals really know how it feels to sit downstairs running yourself though the mental torture chamber of how inadequate you feel as a parent? You simply don't have the right help, support or resources to help you regain control over a child you can't reason with. It's like living in a real-life nightmare, and all you want to do is scream your head off because you feel like you cannot take the frustration of it all anymore.

I would beat myself up, telling myself what a bad parent I was. Then I would have to bath James again, put him downstairs and start scrubbing his room down. It was as if I was having my own childhood tantrum, swearing to myself under my breath while cleaning up and cursing about how much I hated my life!

Maybe you don't like what I'm saying. I'm not sugar-coating it, I'm telling it how it is. I wish my life could be sugar-coated. It's tough, and when you send your child to a specialist school you hope they will meet all your child's needs. It's sad when you realise it's not all it's cracked up to be.

When James got his place at the special needs nursery I thought, *This is it. We're going to get there*. I like to see myself as a very honest person. I put one hundred per cent into everything I do and I don't quit easily, even in the face of the biggest challenges. I am far from perfect, but my children mean the world to me and I will provide anything they need, and that doesn't mean I spoil them.

When James would go to bed after I finished the poo scrubbing, I would spend my time researching autism. I would look to see if it was curable; to see if there was any pioneering medical treatment out there in our big world. Something I did come across that really interested me was a wheat-free and gluten-free diet, and the more I read about it the more hope it gave me in terms of solving the toilet-training and poo-smearing issues.

CHAPTER FOUR

James had been attending the LEA nursery for a few months and toilet-training didn't even seem to be on the radar. He got transport to school, so I didn't see any of the teachers. I could phone, but it was more difficult to catch them at the right time that way. The nappies were going in with him but I had no idea about his progress or what they did with him during the day.

We had a communication diary, but this was only used as a basic messenger, when I needed to send in some cream or more nappies, for example. I was desperate to toilet-train him because the amount of nappies he went through during the day was costing us a fortune, and having to shower him down after he had a bowel movement was a job in itself. In the end, James was assessed by a nurse for free nappies because by his age he should have been toilet-trained and out of them.

James was still eating inedible items, so we had to watch him all the time. On a few occasions after he had been at nursery all week I would have to shower him down on a Saturday morning because it was easier than using individual wipes. I would stand him in the bath, take his nappy off and, to my surprise, the nappy would be shimmering like a Christmas decoration because of all the glitter in his poo. By the looks of things he had eaten a full jar of the stuff. On another occasion the bath was full of sand. It took quite a while to wash it away down the plughole.

This bowel problem was really taking its toll and I was getting fed up with all the work. I had read about leaky gut syndrome on the internet and had bought a book that a boy with Asperger's had written. It was about the gluten-free and casein-free (GFCF) diet (casein is found in all milk products). This lad had brothers who were autistic and they were all on the wheat-free, gluten-free diet.

He is such an inspirational person to have written this book at the age of twelve. I loved it. It was well-written, it gave me hope and it changed a hell of a lot of things in our lives when we did exactly what it said. This book was very useful and it helped me understand a lot about the diet, so it was also very interesting. I did gather information from other sources and they all shared the same fundamental theory.

I found that the information I sourced about wheat, gluten and casein food intolerances all expressed similar concerns. Many children on the autistic spectrum suffer with bowel problems as a result of having these ingredients in their diet. Intolerance to these foods is known as leaky gut syndrome.

The main symptom is either frequent constipation or loose bowels. Other side effects include: a constant craving for foods that are at the root of the problem, behavioural problems, excessive thirst, red ears, poor sleeping patterns, dark circles under the eyes, bloated stomach, pale face and a high pain threshold.

There is evidence to suggest that removing the foods that cause the problems from the diet can have a remarkable impact. There is supposed to be a connection between children on the autistic spectrum having Candida overgrowth in their gut. This makes the gut permeable, which is why it is called leaky gut.

The theory is that if the sufferer has intolerances to wheat, gluten or casein, that person struggles to break down the proteins and they end up as broken peptide chains, which leak through the gut wall and into the blood stream, which causes pain in the stomach. These peptides are known as gluteomorphine from wheat and gluten and casomorphine from casein. As you may have guessed, the word 'morphine' is used here and the side-effects of taking morphine can be very similar. Leaky gut can also cause hyperactivity, unexplained hysterical laughing and a constant desire for the problematic foods.

I read up on this and contacted Philip Teal at the Autism Research Unit, who advised me to cut out the suspect foods separately. So I decided to eliminate casein from his diet first as Philip said this would take the least amount of time to get out of his system. I tried this for around two weeks and it made no difference at all, so I decided to cut all wheat and gluten out of his diet. Philip said James would go through a withdrawal period that usually lasts up to twenty-one days at the most, even though wheat and gluten can stay in the body for up to eight months.

From my experience, wheat and gluten was definitely the culprit. Towards the end of the first week he was off wheat and gluten, I received a call from the nursery. One of the members of staff phoned me to say James hadn't had a bowel movement that day. Well, I was ecstatic. Yes! Yes! I felt this was going to make such a difference and would bring some real improvements to our lives.

The thing is it wasn't easy. James did have withdrawal symptoms, which resulted in more temper tantrums. He had temper tantrums for about eighteen days in all. It was eighteen days of sheer hell, but when the eighteen days were up it was as though the energy around him had changed; something was different. He appeared to be calmer and the frequent loose bowel movements stopped, which meant that the smearing incidents were also less frequent.

I can honestly say with all my heart that if your child is anything like mine, do it. It is well worth it. The problem is that everyone has their own views and people will say that there is not enough medical evidence to support this theory. Fair enough. I did it and, lack of evidence or not, it worked for me.

I will say a few things on the matter. It's not easy at first to do the diet, and if you're putting your child on a wheat-free or gluten-free diet everyone else must follow the same rules, including the school, respite facility, family members and anyone else who has your child, for that matter. In the past, people have said, "Awww, go on. Not even a little bit?" No, not even a little bit. Even just small amounts can really set you back and you can also see a difference in their behaviour. On the occasions when James managed to get hold of any gluten and wheat products, I could tell almost instantly. He would become very hyperactive, running up and down, giggling uncontrollably.

A lot of the time I would be following him about at parties, hovering over him and making sure he didn't eat any foods that contained gluten. Wherever we went with James, we took a packed lunch. Gluten is in everything! It was in all of his favourite foods, so we had to buy everything from the gluten-free range.

The free-from range has its own aisle at the supermarket and there is a good range now that food intolerances have become more common. Or perhaps this is due to the fact that we are better educated nowadays. There is more evidence and research to prove that food allergies and intolerances are real rather than listening to the same old-fashioned opinion that 'kids are allergic to everything these days'. People say: "There wasn't any of this can't eat this and can't have that when we were kids."

When you hear these bold statements it makes you wonder what has changed. Is it all the pesticides we spray our crops with? The meats we buy that are injected with hormones to make them look bigger? And what about all the chemicals in cleaning products and the high pollution levels because we are poisoning ourselves through mass production?

There must be something that is causing us all to become ultra-sensitive to the foods we eat and the environment in which we live. The things I have learnt through having an autistic child have taken me down a different path in life and have given me a mass of knowledge about things I would never have dreamed of beforehand. James has been a real education for me.

Being on a gluten-free diet and buying the biscuits, breadsticks, pasta, cereal, little cakes and bread can be quite expensive. However, James' bowel problems were quite bad, so in the end I ended up getting his food on prescription. There are also recipes out there teaching you how to make your own biscuits and bread.

I must say that I had a go at making soda bread once. It tastes all right, but it was very heavy and rock hard. James wouldn't eat it, so it was pretty much a waste of time. I have made gluten-free cakes before and I once made him a lovely birthday cake that was gluten-free. All my friends loved it and couldn't believe it was gluten-free, but again James didn't eat it. I suppose it was his fussy nature around food.

The beauty about being on a gluten-free diet is that you cannot eat rubbish. It is pretty much a healthy diet, especially if you don't eat all the yummy things James likes. Gluten is in everything that is processed, and sometimes it hides itself under various names: monosodium glutamate, barley, malt, oats, rye, spelt and even vinegar, which has barley in it. So you really need to make sure you read labels carefully.

If you want to eat out and you're on a wheat-free, gluten-free diet, you need to ask and make sure that the foods they are serving are gluten-free. Most menus these days will tell you if they contain certain allergens that are known to cause intolerances or even worse. Some people have allergies that are so bad they cause anaphylactic shock.

The other thing is that if you really like fish and chips from the local chippy, ask if they will cook the fish and the chips separately because if they don't you will end up accidentally ingesting gluten because the batter around the fish contains gluten. Some chippies, like our local, offer gluten-free batter, so it's worth asking. There are books out there about the gluten-free diet and you can get books that tell you where to find restaurants that have a gluten-free range. There is also more than enough information on the internet. At first it seems like a minefield, but eventually you will pick it up and get used to it. It's not so bad.

***

Even though James' bowel movements were less frequent and the smearing wasn't as regular, he did still do it. It was behavioural, but it didn't help matters that he still wasn't toilet-trained. When you have a child with severe communication difficulties and they cannot tell you they when need the toilet it makes the problem worse. The nursery still wasn't making any attempt to toilet-train James and this had become a major issue. James really needed to be toilet-trained, not only because of the smearing issues but because it was getting more and more difficult to change an older boy in public toilets. Plus he needed to retain some dignity.

Other new behaviours were starting to become more of a problem. He found it difficult to cope with change and when he was dropped off by the school bus the temper tantrums came from nowhere. It was like he couldn't cope with the transition from being at school to being on the bus to coming back to the house. James' patience when it came to being on public transport was not good at the best of times, and he would start having a tantrum within a few minutes of being in our car. We were constantly walking on eggshells.

It was confusing trying to work out what would spark him off. All I could put it down to was high anxiety levels. James had no means of telling us what was wrong as he still had no language at all and using any form of PECS symbols to describe the problem was far too complex for him to grasp. The thing I started to do, which I discovered by accident, was that putting some music on and dancing around the living room proved to be a great distraction technique. This seemed to alter his mood fairly quickly.

The number of times I've pranced around the living room to the *Swan Lake* music pretending to be a ballerina! I just wanted to add a bit of humour to the situation and the best thing about it was seeing people walking past the house nosily gawping in with bemused looks on their faces. It was well worth it for that. It's not easy and it's not very funny having a severely autistic child. It is tiring, stressful and emotionally upsetting but sometimes, just sometimes, you have to look for humour!

Don't get me wrong, I don't always see the funny side, especially when I have to deal with a new behaviour and think, *Oh no. How do I deal with this, then?* Then you ring around trying to find a professional person who can give you the tried and tested procedure, but you find they haven't got a clue. Or worse, they give you the wrong advice.

***

Every tantrum resulted in headbanging, and not just a little tap, tap when he was having an episode. This was violent headbanging. It was intentional self-harm with the aim of causing as much damage as possible. His aggression level was so high that people with lower pain barriers would think *Owww! I'm not doing this anymore, it hurts too much.*

Not with James, though. His pain barrier didn't seem to exist at all. He would do it anywhere and on anything. The harder the surface the better it was for him. He would headbang against the car window, the walls, the doors, the floors and even the metal baby gate. The wooden gate social services had fitted for us had a huge crack down the middle and his car headrest had finally broken in two. He had to sit behind the front passenger side because he had axe-kicked me in the shoulder, and we had to replaster the bedroom wall because he had put his head through it.

Watching your child deliberately harming himself with this self-destructive behaviour is one of the hardest, most distressing things to see and deal with. It is absolutely exhausting. Shouting at him didn't work. The only thing we could do was hold him. We would hold him tight so he couldn't move or headbang. It was horrendous. We were so worried he would end up with brain damage or having a stroke, or even going blind. What then? Who is held responsible if that happens?

Trying to get the right help and information on dealing with this behaviour was horrendous, and I was at breaking point. Not only was he doing this during the day, he would also wake up in the middle of the night and do it. I wouldn't let him out of his bedroom at three o'clock in the morning and just let him go downstairs to do whatever he wanted. He was a three-year-old child with severe autism and I'll tell you my thinking behind this. I know there are a lot of parents out there who would let their child go downstairs, and you may think, *This is how my life is and I accept that I can't do anything to change it, so I might as well roll with it.*

The way Dale and I looked at it was that James lives in a world that he doesn't understand, and although we do our best to understand his view of the world, we do not live in James' autistic world. So clear boundaries needed to be set so that he would learn through patterns and routine. I never let James downstairs before 6.30am, and the reason for this was that if I let him go down at two, three or four o'clock in the morning, how would he ever learn to distinguish between acceptable and unacceptable behaviour?

He would have ended up getting up at whatever time he felt like, which would have led to numerous problems: me and Dale not getting enough sleep and being unable to cope with him or day-to-day life, and Dale being unable to work through exhaustion. This could have also put James at risk if one of us had nodded off on the couch in the middle of the night when we were supposed to be supervising him. Our ability to deal reasonably with him would have gone out the window, because we all know that sleep is an essential part of survival. Without sleep the chances of accidents and mistakes are higher, and our general well-being is greatly compromised.

So the tantrums at night would result in me lying on the bed holding him so he couldn't throw his head back. He would be screaming and digging his toes and fingernails into my skin. I would let go of him once his tantrum had ceased. If I had let him go and let him headbang away he probably would have woken the people next door up, and on a few occasions he did, not to mention my fear about the internal damage he was doing to himself.

This was starting to happen more frequently, but not every single night, so it was hard to judge when he was going to kick off. Emotionally and mentally this was becoming more and more difficult to deal with. The panic about his health and the up and down sleep pattern he had was taking its toll.

Added to this, Adam thought he would have a go at the whole headbanging thing, seeing that it sparked off quite a bit of attention. Adam didn't do it for very long, and at nowhere near the force James did, because it hurt too much and he realised it wasn't much fun at all. No amount of negative attention was worth that amount of pain for Adam.

***

I remember Debbie witnessing James' headbanging for herself once. She was watching James while I nipped out to the shops, and it started because she had given him quite a lot of cream crackers and he wanted more. She was shocked by the force with which he was hitting the baby gate with his head, so she gave him the whole pack because she couldn't bear to watch what he was doing to himself any longer.

The more attention he got the worse it grew, and it wasn't something I could ignore any longer. I needed help and I needed it right away. I recall phoning the school to see what they had put in place for this behaviour, and there was nothing. If he had a meltdown they just made sure that he was sitting on the floor and that he wasn't at any further risk of doing damage to himself or anybody else. Then they just let the tantrum take its course.

I knew when he had been headbanging at school because his head would be bruised, or if I looked through his hair at the back of his head his scalp would be bruised and red. Enough was enough, and one day I ended up having a meltdown myself. I felt like my ability to cope and do what was best for James was getting low. I had no direction in terms of the best way to deal with this self-harming behaviour James was displaying.

I ended up phoning Elaine from the children with disabilities team. Her job was to arrange referrals and arrange for James' access services, which provide him with the help he needs. James ended up getting a referral to occupational therapy and they provided a foam helmet that would protect his head. Obviously, this wouldn't prevent any internal damage James might have been subjecting himself to, but it did stop the superficial bruising on his head.

It wasn't the answer, as it didn't work as a deterrent and he hated it. Trying to get a helmet on a child who is having a major meltdown and having to fasten it through a buckle was very difficult, especially when he was fighting with all of his might to stop me putting it on. It was murder. With him screaming and snotting everywhere, and that little bright red face, he was like a raging bull. As the parent I would stand there with my heart racing because I felt as though I had been in a wrestling ring.

The stress this put us under was ridiculous, and the helmet didn't work. James wouldn't think, *Oh, if I nut that baby gate I'm going to end up with the helmet on. I'd best not do it then.* It was a learned behaviour that was deeply ingrained; it was just part of what he did when things weren't going right for him.

I had also been shown a little iceberg sketch of what happens when a child like James loses the plot and how the episode starts at baseline, under the water, like an underlying trigger that kick-starts the temper tantrum. It travels all the way to the top, where the tantrum meets its peak and then slowly starts to diminish as it drops back down to the other side.

This was a great theory, but it didn't really help me out. What do I do in the meantime when this tantrum is manifesting and reaching its peak? It's not so bad if you have a safe space (a room with foam walls) to put children in while they get on with it and scream it out, but we didn't have a safe space to put James in. All we had was his bedroom, and when we put him in there it got torn to pieces bit by bit. There was no structured behavioural plan, there was nothing.

One bit of advice was that when James had a meltdown we should put him on a beanbag. If he kept running over to a wall or to the baby gate to headbang we were to pick him up and put him back on it. I went straight out and bought one to put this advice to the test.

Well, this was a right pain to do and all it did was waste a lot of time. It just added fuel to the fire. I didn't realise this at the time. I didn't understand that the more you turn your attention to a worry or a problem, the bigger it gets. This was exactly what was going on with James. Life is an experience; a massive learning curve. I was young and this child was about to send me on a path of discovery from all angles.

The beanbag didn't work, and although we continued with the helmet it was still a stressful procedure for all of us to go through. One thing I found out was that some children on the autistic spectrum like weighted blankets on them to calm high anxiety levels, so every now and again when James had a meltdown I would wrap him up tight in a duvet and put pressure on his arms and legs. It sounds absurd, but it worked. It was as though the weight reset his emotional response to the world when everything span out of control.

***

While all this was going on we had been referred to the behavioural team. When our appointment finally came through, the therapist came over for a home visit. The first visit involved an observation to see what was going on, and during the second visit they explained their findings and talked about how to deal with certain behavioural patterns.

One of the suggestions was that I should give him scraps when cooking, for example bits of salad. The problem was that he had already had a snack before they got to the house and I don't agree with filling children up with too many snacks before they have tea, especially when they already have food aversions. The second piece of advice was to take turns playing games of KerPlunk. This was written out and stuck to the fridge for a while, but to be honest the service we were receiving for James was poor. It was amateur!

I couldn't take it anymore and neither could Dale. That was it. We had had enough of the local authority's attempts to educate and help our child, and of them trying to help us as parents, not to mention various professionals advising us to go on positive parenting courses. I had been on every single course going! When you're told to go on a positive parenting course it's an insult to your intelligence and I was sick of hearing the phrase, "It's not meant like that!"

To the ones who think we were being pig-headed, thinking, *What's another course? It's just another hoop. What's another appointment, for that matter?* The thing is, the professionals think you only have an appointment with them. They don't realise how many others you have to attend.

The last time an OT advised me to go on a positive parenting course, the response was: "You go on the course, then have James for two weeks and let me know how your positive parenting turns out!" It was a game of biding our time and jumping through hoops. We'd had enough! Things weren't improving and no amount of courses could patch things up and make everything better.

CHAPTER FIVE

By this time, James had been at the LEA nursery for two years. It was time for him to start reception class and things weren't getting any easier at all. In fact, things were getting worse and James was showing no signs of improvement. The pressure we were under as a family was immense. We decided to look for specialist help for James, so Dale and I looked at non-LEA maintained schools in the hope that they would be able to help James develop educationally and socially.

We had also looked at one LEA school. The head said the school wouldn't take James on because of the severity of his autism. We looked at two other schools that specialised in autism. Although they sounded very good, we kept hearing through the grapevine about how well applied behaviour analysis (ABA) therapy worked for autistic children.

Dale's accountant Miles had a couple of clients whose children were on the autistic spectrum and their children had been receiving ABA therapy.

Miles gave us a contact number for one of these clients, who spoke about the therapy in glowing terms. He told us how his child's speech had progressed at an accelerated rate, and how well and how far his child had come.

It sounded too good to be true. It was like all our prayers had been answered at once and everything we had wished for was within reach, especially when we found out that one of Miles' employees had a nephew who went to an ABA school that was only half an hour away from where we lived. We looked on the internet straightaway and started to research the school. We contacted the owner, Denise, to find out more about how the school operated and she suggested coming in for a visit, adding that it would be a good idea for us to bring James. We couldn't believe it! We were so excited.

When we turned up at the ABA school, it was like a huge house. We were greeted at the front door by an ABA therapist. We waited for a few moments while they let Denise know we were there. The manager, who was also an ABA therapist, was called Faye. She started to show us around and one of the first rooms we went into was an observation room.

By this point James wasn't in the best of moods and his behaviour had started to escalate. Faye said it would be a good idea to get a member of staff to look after James to distract him from having a tantrum. This would also give them the chance to get to know him and we would be able to talk and ask questions about the school.

We had a look around all the classrooms. The house was massive, with a huge garden. The rooms were designated to one child only and each had everything the child needed in it, including toys and learning materials. After we had looked around we went to Denise's office to discuss how the school worked and what the admission criteria was.

While we were in Denise's office we could hear James carrying on. He was having a full-scale meltdown. This sort of behaviour wasn't unusual to us as it happened on a regular basis, which is why we were there looking around the school. Our child was out of control, and still to this day we say that his behaviour was so extreme it was like he was feral.

We were worrying a little at this point as to whether or not the school could handle him. But Denise was the mother of an autistic child and her child attended the school. She assured us that they had dealt with worse, which was pretty hard to get our heads around because James was really extreme at the time. We desperately needed help.

The school sounded fabulous when Denise explained the set-up. Each individual student received one-to-one therapy and each team consisted of four therapists. They had four therapists on each team so that the student didn't get too attached to a particular therapist or to their teaching style. Students needed to be able to adapt to all teaching styles, which would prove that they had mastered the skills they had been taught.

Each student had his or her own designated room. As well as the existing contents, personal belongings and toys would be introduced to be used as reinforcers during the teaching. A reinforcer is used as a reward that the student works for. It is normally a high motivator; something a child really wants and will work hard to have in their possession, even if it's only for a few minutes.

Denise explained that every student is assessed and a personal educational plan is then tailor-made to the child's needs. The ABA programme concentrates on the child's level and ability. It doesn't just educate them in a fast, progressive way; it also works on any negative behaviour that may be inappropriate and destructive to their development and to those around them. The ABA programme also works on life skills. Not just the day-to-day educational things, but how to function properly in society.

It might sound ridiculous to people who don't know a lot about autism, but what Dale and I discovered very quickly, especially because our son is so severely affected, is that while we learn naturally and pick things up very quickly, James couldn't do this. Life skills and dealing with life in general wasn't obvious to him. He had to learn everything from scratch and he had to be taught things over and over again before he mastered a certain skill.

This is why Dale and I were so ecstatic about the

whole ABA programme. We knew this was what James needed in order to cope. Also, the school holidays were minimal. Normal local authority school holidays were seventeen to nineteen weeks per year. The ABA school gave ten days off at Christmas, two weeks in the summer and bank holidays. That was it.

This sounded brilliant as it meant I wouldn't need any respite care at home or respite help during the holidays, and I could go back to work if I wanted to. I could get a normal childminder for Adam when he was off because he was mainstream and wasn't a problem developmentally. The whole thing sounded too good to be true; we were amazed. It was like we could finally see light at the end of the tunnel.

Denise told us that the only problem we had was trying to convince the LEA to give him a funded placement. Going on past experience, this was not going to be easy. She handed us a prospectus with all the information about costs and how the school worked.

By the time we had finished our meeting with

Denise, James had calmed down and seemed to be in a better mood. Dale and I were so happy that there was finally a chance of getting some proper help for James. It was like a dream come true. At last we could start to look forward to the future and this stressful situation could all come to an end. At least, that's what we thought.

***

We had arranged another visit to the ABA school. This time it was for James to be assessed by the school's educational psychologist. His assessment showed that even though James was four, his mental age was that of a two-year-old.

The next phase of the visit took place in the classroom, and this gave us our first taste of ABA therapy. There were two small chairs facing each other with a small table next to them. The ABA educational psychologist, his team, James, Dale and I attended the demonstration. The ABA psychologist sat on one of the small chairs and called James over to sit on the one facing him. James sat down.

There were two large Duplo bricks on the table and a bucket on the floor. The psychologist looked at James, took a brick and threw it into the bucket. He put his hand on top of James' hand and guided it to the table. Then he said: "James do same."

James did the same and the psychologist said, "Well done." He gave James a bit of broken biscuit and told him to go and take a break. James ran around for a few minutes and then the psychologist called him back to his seat. James co-operated straightaway. The psychologist repeated the action and this time James did it without any hand guidance. Wow, we were so amazed! We were amazed that James had followed basic instruction and amazed that he imitated an action. Imitation was a skill he had lost at ten months old, so you can imagine how blown away we were with it all.

Dale and I had already had dealings with the LEA. They knew we weren't happy with James' school placement due to the lack of progress he had made. We had already been to endless meetings, but when Dale spoke to an education officer on the phone and explained our situation and the school placement we had found, they gave us a glimmer of hope. We were offered an appointment with the head education officer.

Dale was very firm. He told them: "If you're going to tell me no, then you can you just do that over the phone, because I don't want to waste more time and take another day off work for a comfort meeting to be told something you can say over the phone."

She said this wouldn't necessarily be the case, and Dale replied with: "So, if you're not saying an out and out *no*, there's a chance the LEA will fund James at the ABA school?"

We booked an appointment to see the head education officer the following week.

***

I had already started looking into going back to work and had a childminder, Louise, lined up to have James. She told me she had experience working with children on the autistic spectrum, so she was happy to take him on. Louise was ready to have James on the Monday while we were at the meeting trying to convince the LEA to fund James' placement at the ABA school.

It seemed to take forever for Monday to come around. When it did we dropped James off at Louise's house and headed off to the council offices. Dale and I were sitting there, waiting in anticipation for the education officer, Joanne Mooney, to come down and collect us from the waiting room. When she did, she took us into a meeting room to meet the head education officer, Sharon Steely.

We sat down, and just before we started talking about the ABA school in detail, Dale asked if anyone was going to take minutes. Dale had worked for the council, and meetings were something he took part in on a regular basis, so he knew this was standard procedure.

He was aghast when Sharon said: "Oh, we don't take minutes in meetings."

"Oh really," was Dale's reply. "How will we remember what has and hasn't been agreed if you don't take any minutes?" He was appalled, and insisted that minutes were taken seeing as we were discussing such a sensitive and important subject.

We started the meeting by explaining the structure of the ABA school, what was involved and how well ABA therapy would work for James' progress. We explained that he was really far behind and still couldn't speak. He was Four years old and still incontinent. We explained that if James got the correct help at this point he would have a much better chance of living an independent life when he was older.

Also, because there weren't many school holidays it meant that we would not need as much respite care either. We knew then that James needed to be taught on a one-to-one basis and that he needed intensive specialist therapy. This was his chance. Joanne sat and took the minutes while we talked about the benefits of James attending the ABA school and how much it would improve his and our quality of life.

When we finished explaining, Sharon said: "Well, I'm telling you now he won't be going to that school!"

I can't tell you how stunned we were by her flippant, cold-hearted reply. All we could see was our son gaining at least a chance of surviving in this world and somebody who didn't have a clue what it was like to live with a severely autistic child had already made up her mind.

This got mine and Dale's backs up straightaway. For one, Dale had already told them we didn't want another time wasting meeting and they had offered us this glimmer of hope only to cruelly retract it. Sharon's argument was that her experience of ABA therapy was that it only had a fifty per cent success rate. Dale asked what this that based on and she replied that she knew of two children who had had ABA therapy.

Dale and I thought this was laughable. Her entire experience of ABA therapy was based on two children. It had worked for one and hadn't for the other. Based on this, our child was being denied a therapy, an education, which would be absolutely paramount for him. The other thing they argued with us was about costs. We couldn't see what the problem was because fewer holidays and less respite meant there wouldn't be a big difference in terms of cost.

The meeting came to an end, and to say that we were annoyed was an understatement. The worst part is being told that the only school your child can attend is the one they dictate, and that you have no other choice. You feel powerless, like people are playing God with your life. There is no reasoning or compromise. Often there isn't even any discussion.

***

We had been at the meeting for two-and-a half hours, so we went straight to the childminder's to pick James up. When we arrived at Louise's house she seemed very upset and James wasn't there. She couldn't apologise enough.

She said: "I'm so sorry, Dale. I had to call your mum and dad to collect him. I couldn't look after him any longer."

Ironically, while we had been at the meeting pleading for the correct help for our child, James had been creating absolute chaos at the childminder's house. Apparently, he had shaken the hamster cage upside down, and kicked and attacked the other children in the house. Louise's husband had been permanently stood by the fridge with his hand on the door trying to stop James emptying the contents. Once he had a quest to do something he wouldn't give up.

In the end, she had been forced to phone Dale's parents to come and collect him because his behaviour was so bad. I couldn't blame her really; who was I kidding about going back to work? That was also looking very bleak. All this episode proved was that we desperately needed the correct help. It strengthened my case even more that this was not down to my parenting, because even at this stage I still blamed myself.

Dale and I started to go over what we needed to do next. We phoned Denise at the ABA school to inform her about the meeting. She wasn't surprised. She explained that James could attend on a sponsorship, which meant that Dale and I would have to pay a monthly fee for James to attend the ABA school. This would cover payment for the staff, any reports that were written and the running of his ABA programmes by the educational psychologist.

The school was a charity, so there was a pot of money to fund sponsorship placements for children while the parents took the local authorities to a tribunal in the hope that they would win funding for a full-time ABA placement. In order to fight the LEA we needed to start collecting evidence and presenting a case against the LEA to show why James needed to be educated at an ABA school.

Even though it was obvious to us that the special needs school had had James for two years and he still hadn't made any progress, we knew this would not stand up on its own at a tribunal. We were advised that we would need a solicitor and various private assessments to show that James needed full-time ABA therapy as part of his education.

This was a big decision for me and Dale to make, because even though James had been offered a sponsorship it was still going to be very costly for us and the only person pulling in a wage was Dale. I tried to look again at going back to work, but I couldn't get a childminder that was specialised enough to deal with James.

We really did some contemplating about James attending the ABA school, but the unease about him not getting ABA therapy wouldn't leave me alone. I phoned Dale at work and told him I had a strong gut feeling that if James didn't go to the school we would be making the biggest mistake of our lives. Dale said that he had the same feeling. So we agreed that I would phone Denise and tell her James could start attending the school as soon as possible. I was so pleased, because deep down I knew it was the right decision.

***

Once this was finalised it was time to get the ball rolling. James was due to start in August because the school only took two weeks off in the summer. This gave me time to organise all the independent professionals we needed to assess James. Dale and I hired a solicitor, an educational psychologist, a psychiatrist, an OT and a speech and language therapist. James was also assessed by the ABA school's educational therapist on a regular basis to monitor his base rate and his progress during this period.

The assessments carried out by the school's ABA psychologist were part of an ongoing service the school provided. Every child was treated the same way, because this school wanted results. It was a successful way of proving that ABA therapy worked well for autistic children. The proof was right there.

We had another appointment at the ABA school before James was due to start so we could see his new classroom and be introduced to his team. His anxiety levels were already high when we went into the classroom and he was having a screaming temper tantrum. However, this soon started to dissolve when he saw the shelves packed with all sorts of toys.

The whole team was there to start work with him: four therapists and the school's educational psychologist. But because James was in a new environment and there were so many new delights in the room he wanted to explore and this took priority over anything else. The team found it very difficult to interact with James that day because he was so distracted by everything in the room. Well that's James for you! He's very inquisitive to say the least.

He wasn't fussed about blending in socially, but he was attracted to everything visually. It's that much of a sensory overload for James that it becomes obsessional and he has to succeed in getting the item he wants and stim with it (stimming is a repetitive action like opening and shutting doors or lining toy cars up). If anybody interrupts or restricts this pattern of behaviour it can result in a meltdown.

If you look at this from a non-autistic adult's point of view, it can get quite irritating if we have a task to do or are reading a really good book and someone keeps interrupting our flow. Well before adulthood we learn to control our temper tantrums when outside influences restrict and prevent us doing what we want to do. When someone is on the autistic spectrum, this focus and drive is at double force. James' sensory overload is so intense he uses objects to block out the outside world. To him, everything else is meaningless. I knew there and then that the multiple stimuli in the room were going to be a problem.

A lot of professionals think ASD parents don't have a clue, whereas they have a degree. However, we soon catch up through personal experience. This experience confirmed to us that James needed a one-to-one educational setting in a low-stimulus environment. We had known this for a long time, but this is where parents' opinions go unacknowledged. Often we are treated as though we are being difficult.

When we realised this school could provide for all of James' needs there was no letting go. We had to move forward and fight. Otherwise, it would be a lifetime of lost hope and despair. Dale and I were not made of the soft stuff and we are especially firm when it comes to fairness and equality. Why should we and our child not have the same chance in life as everyone else?

This was not a lifestyle choice. These were the cards we had been dealt and we were trying to make the best out of the situation. Some people might think we should have let sleeping dogs lie; that's the way he was born, so let him be. You're entitled to your opinion and we're entitled to ours, and we didn't and don't want to institutionalise our child in the future. That would have been heartbreaking.

Some people would see that as the easy option, and sometimes when things have been tough I have thought that myself, although I'm ashamed to admit it. At times life has been unbearable, but I couldn't live with myself if I did that. And I'm not condemning others who have done this, because I understand how difficult the whole situation is. We knew this child had potential and because life was difficult we wanted and needed this ABA therapy for James.

***

We were advised to go to the LEA school for evidence-based reasons as to why we thought this school could not meet James' needs. We had a look at the class they wanted James to go in. Bear in mind that James couldn't speak, had a very low tolerance to sitting still and couldn't even grasp what you were saying to him on a one-to-one basis, never mind in a group setting.

Dale and I visited the LEA school to see how the classroom operated. The class had ten children, two teaching assistants and one teacher. Dale and I sat in on one of the lessons. It lasted about half an hour and the topic was Mother's Day.

A few of the children were getting stressed because they couldn't deal with sitting in a class environment and being taught a subject that meant nothing to them whatsoever. One child was strapped into a chair, and every time he moved his hand slightly one of the teaching assistants sitting either side of him would put his hand back down.

While we were speaking to the teacher after the lesson we noticed one child playing with a small spinning top. He span it over and over again for the remainder of our visit, which lasted another half-hour. Our findings made us even more determined not to send James to the LEA school. The classroom environment was too noisy and too busy. There was a toaster and a kettle within reach of the children and the cupboards were full of snacks. Things were simply too accessible for James and we deemed it unsafe.

We were also left wondering why that child had been restrained in a chair. We knew James was hard work and we didn't want this happening to our son. Then there was the child who was left with his spinning top for half an hour, and the topic of Mother's Day. You may be thinking, *What's wrong with teaching a child about Mother's Day? It's something they need to learn, right?*

Wrong! With children who are severely autistic it seems more beneficial to teach them to speak properly as well as basic life skills, such as the skill of imitating. Teaching them about a subject that is meaningless to them is like putting an English person in a class and being taught a foreign language at an advanced level. How can you teach on a seasonal subject when the kids don't even have basic understanding? It's pointless!

CHAPTER SIX

I remember James' first day at the ABA school. I picked him up at three o'clock and on the way home he fell asleep. *That's good*, I thought, because James never fell asleep in the car. He always had far too much energy for that. They must have worked him really hard for him to fall asleep like that. James had stopped having afternoon naps when he was a toddler, so I took this as a positive sign.

I asked them how he had got on, and they said he had had a great day and that they had managed with him really well. As I had anticipated, they had stripped the room down to the bare minimum to get him to participate in the ABA therapy. All the toys were too much of a distraction for him. The plan was to gradually introduce them so that it wasn't so overwhelming for him.

Every day I was given home sheets with a record of what he had done during the day and which ABA programmes they had worked on with him. The other thing I decided to do was keep a diary of James' progress at the ABA school. My intention was not to write a book about James, but to collect evidence about his progress in case it was needed at the tribunal.

The first time I recorded significant progress with James was within the first two weeks. Before James started there we had a static caravan in North Wales for two years. We had spent a lot of time there because he was so hyper and we had to walk him for miles just to bring his energy levels down. Added to this, James loves the sea and the sand; he gets great pleasure from playing on the beach.

The problems we had were the high anxiety levels in the car, when James would go into meltdown mode. He would react by kicking, screaming and headbanging the windows and the seats. This was a major problem for us because it happened on ninety-five per cent of car journeys and it is incredibly stressful. The following diary entries record a change in this behaviour.

Friday 19th September, 2008

Dale and I took James and Adam to the caravan. It's usually very stressful trying to keep James occupied and happy, as he normally headbangs all the way there. James has been at the ABA school for a full two weeks now and he's like a totally different child. He's more contented and less bad-tempered, to say the least. For the first time in years we didn't feel like we were treading on eggshells.

James had one little temper tantrum all weekend and that was on the Saturday afternoon at the Early Learning Centre because there was a toy he wanted that he couldn't have. But he was easily distracted and soon forgot all about it. He has been fantastic in the car for all the journeys we've been on and we haven't had a single outburst. This was a fantastic improvement for us because we hadn't seen James this calm since he was a baby, and he was four years old by this time.

Whatever the local authority was providing in terms of James' education and support it wasn't working, and we had first-hand experience of this. It was amazing to see this progress. Within two weeks of receiving ABA therapy, a big problem like this was becoming more manageable. The relief from his problem behaviour was like respite in itself, even though this was only the very tip of the iceberg. It really gave us hope and a new sense of strength for the future.

James had stopped waving goodbye when he was ten months old. This was something I had really paid attention to when it happened. I remember feeling confused by this, but I decided to put it to the back of my mind and subconsciously I thought that he might start doing it again when he was ready. When people were leaving the house and I waved goodbye to them he didn't even look at them. He was always more interested in looking past them at something else.

James had no interest in people at all. He wouldn't pay attention to them, so you couldn't get him to imitate gestures. This was why he didn't progress and learn human behaviour. No matter how many times we tried to get him to look he just wouldn't look. It was as though they were invisible, like ghosts even, and because they weren't part of his world he had no interest in interacting with them.

Even if I pointed to things like animals to share experiences with him he wasn't interested. I didn't know he was autistic at this age, when these little problems started to arise. I just thought he was more interested in other things and that he would catch up when he was ready. I put it to the back of my mind and we just got on with our lives.

James was four by this point and he still couldn't wave goodbye. Here's what I wrote five weeks into the ABA therapy.

Friday 24th October, 2008

I took James to the chemist today and he waved goodbye to the pharmacist. The last time I saw him do this he was around ten months old. I also took him to a hairdressing appointment. The last time I took him to a hairdressing appointment he was a little baby. He was so well-behaved!

It was like having a new independence and freedom. We were able to do the normal things other families do instead of having to arrange for family members to babysit so we could attend appointments. The progress he was making seemed to be coming on thick and fast. It was a delight to see that my severely autistic son could be taught social and life skills and that, as well as learning them at school, he was applying them in the real world.

The reality started to hit home that one day it might be possible for our child to have some independence later on in life. It gave us the glimmer of hope we had been waiting to see. It backed up the gut feeling we had always had: that if you keep plugging away and tick off each new mastered skill from the list, one day our child would have the skills to live either an independent or a semi-independent life rather than being institutionalised.

The more skills and understanding they gain the less vulnerable they are. Other things were also starting to come into play. It was like he was developing a new consciousness of the world around him; something he had never had before. He was becoming more aware of other people, rather than them simply being objects to him or a means of getting what he needed. He was beginning to interact more appropriately with people.

Tuesday 28th October, 2008

I spoke to my dad on the phone today and asked Adam if he wanted to speak to Granddad Bob. James snatched the phone off me. He just held it to his ear and listened. Usually James has no interest at all in the telephone; in fact there have been many occasions when I have tried to get James to use the phone but he would always push it away. I couldn't believe it, it was amazing. This might not sound like much, but it's a massive step forward for James. This showed me that he wanted to be involved and to interact with others rather than being trapped in his autistic world.

Another skill James was taught at the ABA school was toilet-training. I had tried to toilet-train James myself at home but had failed miserably because his previous school wouldn't train him within the school setting. You find that if people around you are not consistent in their approach and don't do the same things as you, it makes things extremely difficult. This doesn't just go for toilet-training, it works across the board: rules and boundaries, special diets, restricted objects, behavioural rules, everything!

Consistency is the key with children, especially children who are on the autistic spectrum. Through our experience, we found that the more consistent people were the fewer meltdowns we saw. The way I see it, James is severely autistic and has a hard time figuring things out as it is. By keeping things clear and consistent, James knew where he stood, which reduced his anxiety levels. We found that behaviours would flare up if there was a weak link and someone wasn't sticking to the plan. There are no grey areas with autistic children; there is only black and white. This is why they don't really understand this idiom. With everyone working together, this became more and more apparent.

If the school your child goes to teaches ABA therapy, family, friends and the respite setting must do likewise. We found that behavioural issues were at a minimum because everyone was running a tight ship and James' world was a less confusing place to be in because he knew what acceptable and unacceptable behaviour was.

To avoid any confusion, the ABA school always made sure skills were mastered in the school setting before we were allowed to do them at home. The skills James was mastering were expressed at the monthly meetings we attended. This was done so that we could keep the new skills maintained at home and apply them in day-to-day life.

Here's what happened within eight weeks of him being at the ABA school:

Wednesday 5th November, 2008

James independently started to use the potty of his own accord today. He has done this three times today. I went up to his bedroom and he was sitting on the potty. He had done a poo. I had no involvement in this at all; he had done it himself.

James has been able to copy me making the sound of 'ooo' today! He can also imitate us by chattering his teeth, blowing raspberries and stamping his feet.

This progress was absolutely amazing! The problems and the stress I had had with James smearing and flinging poo around the bedroom looked like they were finally coming to an end.

James sitting on the potty without being requested to by anyone was such a wonderful thing because it showed massive leaps of progress in such a short space of time. It proved that our child had huge potential and backed up the view we already had of James. This gave us proof that he could be taught and gave us huge hope for the future. The skills he was learning so intensively and quickly in his new educational setting were being applied in the real world.

I know there are a lot of people out there who don't like ABA therapy. Some people have even suggested that it is a cruel therapy, and that children on the autistic spectrum should be accepted for the way they are and left alone. People have claimed that ABA therapy is cruel because it is like a form of dog training.

I think most people care more for animals than they do for their fellow human beings, so if dog training was that cruel it would be banned. For me, ABA therapy is about working on a particular skill repeatedly for a small reward over a short period of time. If this works for a child like James, this proves that ABA is a powerful therapy. It works by unlocking their true potential. It was opening him up to a world that didn't make any sense to him before, making it more accessible bit by bit.

The way I see it is that we don't live in an autistic world, and to get on in this world we have to learn new skills and evolve. That's just part of life. Even those of us that are not autistic go through a lifetime of learning skills; we are forever learning. We don't say, "Well I'm not sending my child to school because being educated is cruel."

I don't think it can ever be right to put a cap on anyone's potential. I don't believe in that kind of negativity; that's the kind of view I will not accept. Many times professionals have sat in my front room for some kind of review and have asked me if I'm expecting too much of him. I can tell you, it gets my back right up. Who are they to sit there and judge? Who are they to discourage me, to trample on my hopes for my child's future? This shows the narrow-mindedness and low expectations these children are surrounded by. It's no wonder people lose sight and hope.

Other progress James was making was becoming more and more apparent. The skills he was learning at the ABA school were shining through and he was applying them in everyday life. It showed that he was soaking these new skills up like a sponge and he was doing it independently. There were no prompts from any adults, he just did it naturally.

One of the therapists on his ABA team told me and Dale that she had been teaching ABA therapy for ten years and that she had never seen a child as ready and willing to learn as he is. She said that as soon as he had his reward he would be straight back to the table ready to learn. She told us James seemed to love learning.

Saturday 22nd November, 2008

I was talking to my gran today on the phone. I

gave Adam the phone so that he could speak to her. James was standing there and he looked so interested, like he wanted to join in. So I passed the phone to James and he made all the sounds the ABA school had been teaching him down the phone. You could tell by his little face that he was putting his whole heart into it.

Teaching James sounds, noises and phonics were all part of his ABA programme. This was all in preparation for teaching him how to speak, and by the looks of things it was starting to work. They also did facial imitation exercises with him, so he had to watch intently to get this right. This was done to strengthen the muscles in his face and around his mouth, because if a person has never spoken before these muscles are very weak. This can affect the way the person talks and can even make trying to imitate someone else difficult.

Monday 24th November, 2008

I was running late taking James to school this morning, so when we arrived his team was waiting for us in reception. They noticed he had

had his hair cut. The girls said, "Awww, look at him, he's had his hair cut. He looks dead cute!"

The funny thing is, James went all shy and buried his head in his lunch box. This definitely shows he has a good understanding for him to go all shy the way he did, but it's still not tangible with him. There are still a lot of things he doesn't understand, so the whole process can be very confusing and it's hard to judge. Some things seem obvious and we're sure he'll get them, but he won't, while the things we think he won't understand he often does.

Thursday 27th November, 2008

I poured Adam some milk and gave James some water. James made it very clear to me with sounds and gestures that what he really wanted was milk.

I asked him: "Does James want milk?"

James nodded at me.

"Say 'yes'," I said.

James nodded again and then said "Yep!" I got him to repeat it a second time to check that it wasn't a fluke and that he was consistent in his response. A while later James did the same for Dale. We are going to keep this up over the weekend. He is really trying.

Friday 28th November, 2008

I have a lady who comes round to the house on a Friday night to give us respite. Her name is Andrea and she is lovely. She is kind and patient with James, and she is also very reliable.

Tonight we went out and when we came back Andrea told us they had played non-stop while we were out, building towers and then knocking them down. She told us how well he was doing because he was initiating his own play. He would also go and give her a cuddle every now and then. She was amazed by James' progress because she has been working with him for quite some time, and at one time he wouldn't interact with her through play.

Saturday 29th November, 2008

Today we had meeting at our house for James to undergo his first private assessment in terms of collecting evidence to be used at the tribunal. The two women Joan and Audrey came round and jointly assessed James. One was a SALT and the other was an OT. The reason I have added this entry into the diary is because it is relevant in terms of James' behaviour.

At one time, Dale and I had a bit of a problem keeping James' clothes on. He would strip off a lot and he didn't really care where he did it. This was due to his autism, which affected his social awareness levels. At home we tended to keep a potty in every room while James was toilet-training.

When Joan and Audrey arrived we sat in the back living room, where one of James' potties was. He came in, took the potty and carried it into the kitchen. This was a really good sign, because it proved he was starting to gain some awareness.

A bit later on, before Joan and Audrey left, James started to have some behavioural issues. I had to put him in his bedroom for time out with his helmet on because he had started to headbang. When James had calmed down I went upstairs to get him, and because he had worked himself up into such a state he had wet himself. He had no pants on, but when I went to take him downstairs he quickly picked up his pyjama bottoms and put them on. This might not sound like a big deal, but it is. It proves that James is starting to gain some social concepts.

Sunday 30th November, 2008

James woke up early this morning. He had done a poo on the potty, put his own nappy back on and sat nicely waiting for his dad.

He kept trying to climb on the easel, so I told James if he did it again I would take his banana away from him. James stood there grinning, shaking his head. It was a clear no!

Saturday 13th December, 2008

James brought a pink plastic piggy bank downstairs. He sat on the kitchen floor and posted the big pink plastic coins into it. He did this for a few minutes. I have never seen James playing with a toy in the correct way before, let alone doing it off his own bat. Amazing!!!

Tuesday 20th January, 2009

Adam and I were colouring in on the floor with a wipeable book. James came over and sat there for more than five minutes. He was colouring each page and turning the pages over. This is wonderful progress to see.

Thursday 22nd January, 2009

James was walking around the living room today with a little book and looking at all the pictures.

Thursday 29th January, 2009

Adam's craft scissors and paper were left out on the table today, and James went over to the table and started cutting with them.

Sunday 1st February, 2009

Today I spoke to James over the phone. He recognised my voice and he said "Ma".

Tuesday 3rd February, 2009

Tonight we took James and Adam to a big indoor soft play area with an autism support group. James wanted a Kit Kat from the shop. I explained to him that he couldn't have one because he was on a gluten-free diet, but that next time we went there I would bring his biscuits. I told him to have an apple. He decided to have a banana instead, and was very happy with that. Usually he has a huge tantrum when he's denied something, but I think his understanding of language is getting a lot better; even better than we realise.

Wednesday 11th February, 2009

James leant over the gate tonight to reach for his Visual Timetable. He took the timetable and then came back to the gate. Then he showed me the picture of the bath and said, "Bath". I couldn't believe it. I'm so excited!!!

Tuesday 10th February, 2009

I was playing music in the car on the way to school, and when I looked in the rear view mirror I saw James dancing, shaking his wrists

about. I spoke to one his ABA tutors about it and she said that was one of the aerobics moves they had been teaching him at school through his imitation programme.

James was using all the new skills he was learning outside of the educational setting. It was an absolute joy to see him initiating play, and even the fact that he was able to hear my voice and know who I was displayed brilliant recognition.

In March 2009 I had written a list of all the skills James had learnt through ABA therapy. I had written this list because the tribunal was approaching and this was my own personal evidence for James. We had all this evidence well documented through continuous assessments and anyone could see that ABA therapy was our preferred educational teaching method. The progress was so evident for all to see. The tribunal was due to take place on Monday 23rd March, 2009.

March 2009

James is using his PECS book consistently now.

James will go to the easel unprompted and draw with chalk.

James is now using syllables.

James is now more accepting when people take items away from him.

James waves bye-bye and blows kisses.

James is more tolerant when he has to wait for something.

James will tolerate us cutting up food items on his plate.

James will kick a football back and forth to another person.

May 2010

James can ride a bike.

James can imitate almost anything you say.

James can use a lot of words unprompted.

James can ask for items using speech.

James hardly has tantrums now.

James is dry at night.

James has more of an interest in toys.

All this progress I had recorded was just the tip of

the iceberg. He was coming on by leaps and bounds in all areas. When James first started his ABA therapy he was only working on six programmes at a time. This soon went up to fifteen programmes. With James making this much progress it really felt as though ABA therapy was some kind of wonder drug. It made life so much more bearable for us as a family.

The only thing we needed to do was present this evidence to the tribunal. Seeing that we had such great evidence and all the private assessments we had done backed them up, strengthening James' case, there shouldn't have been any problem winning the tribunal and getting the LEA to pay for James' education.

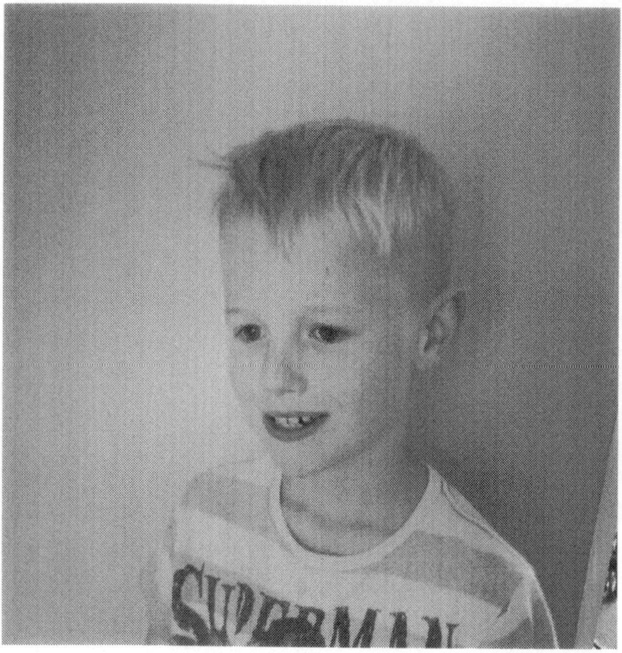

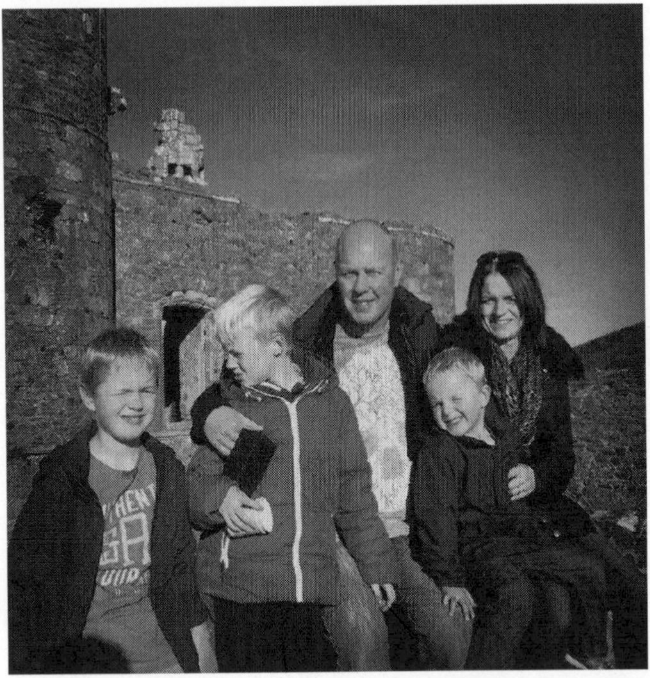

CHAPTER SEVEN

One of James' first assessments was carried out by Victoria Fone. Victoria was an experienced educational psychologist, with more than thirty years of experience. Dale and I employed Victoria to carry out a private assessment, which would be used as part of the tribunal evidence. Victoria first assessed James on the 29th August, 2008, prior to James starting at the ABA school. The aim was to show James' baseline at the time, while further assessments would be good evidential indicators of any progress James made.

The first assessment Victoria carried out on James went into great detail on a range of problems James experiences because his autism is so severe. The assessment reported how difficult it was to get James to sit down and show any interest in toys. James was also tested for symbolic play and failed this test because he had none.

Victoria went on to say that James was extremely active and would rush across the room to take things out of the kitchen cupboard. She also observed how limited James' concentration span was. Victoria said that James' most severe characteristic was his inability to communicate. At the time James was four years old and his communication skills were below the two-year-old level. She also noted that he avoided eye contact and tended to play with toys inappropriately.

Victoria added that James demonstrated some understanding of simple situation commands, especially when one or two phrases were used. He did not always comply, but it was clear that he understood. Victoria also stated that James did not have any meaningful spoken words, although he did babble.

Victoria noticed that James used the word 'apple', but that this was not very clear and that he used the word generically. He was able to use PECS symbols but at a very basic level, and Victoria felt this could be extended considerably. James was at the average level of a three-year-old for eating, dressing and undressing. James was not toilet-trained at the time of the assessment. He did wee on the potty when asked, but there were ongoing problems with smearing faeces.

She noted that:

James could not imitate and did not understand instructions.

James couldn't wave goodbye.

James was able to climb, run and jump, but it did not appear that he could hop.

James would sit on a tricycle and peddle backwards, but he couldn't peddle forwards.

James did not like eye contact and did not interact well, although he did allow other children to join in when he was playing.

Victoria stated in the report that James was capable of learning and acquiring these skills, and that he could be developed further. She said that James liked music but that she had not had any success with him while singing, "Head, Shoulders, Knees and Toes". He did not join in with this activity.

It was reported in the assessment that James did not like any changes in routine and that he didn't follow rules, but other reports suggested that he coped better in a structured, controlled environment.

Victoria concluded her assessment with a list of recommendations. She said that James' autism and his very limited attention span prevented him from learning, but that he had demonstrated that he can be taught to request items using PECS.

She wrote that James displayed high levels of demand avoidance, although he was highly motivated by food rewards and by praise. She explained that James also ran around and sought distractions, even in environments containing minimal distractions.

Victoria noted that James' main strength was his visual skills, although his attention span was a problem. She said that James would need to be in a quiet, structured setting so that he could focus on the tasks he was being taught. She added that he would need an intensive individual teaching programme with development curricula. Victoria stated that he required a clear programme to develop the ability to communicate his needs through PECS and to help understand, request and be informed of what was happening using visual clues.

She suggested a small steps approach, learning discrete trial teaching, which means that a skill is taught in broken down steps and then built up by applying the teaching methods of ABA therapy. Victoria said that a similar approach should be used to modify unwanted behaviour and to encourage reward compliance.

Victoria said that it was important that strategies were recorded so that James' progression through ABA therapy could be evaluated. She said that he would continue to need help from a SALT and an OT. Any strategies that were used within his educational setting would need to be demonstrated to us so that he could generalise these new skills in the home and community.

She agreed to review James' in approximately three months' time.

Further addendum to the psychologist report

13th December, 2008

This assessment was carried out at the ABA school.

Victoria noted that James' symbolic play had improved slightly but that it was still severely delayed. When toys were presented to him he did show some interest. The toy set that was presented to him consisted of a tractor, a trailer, some logs and a man. James put the logs in his mouth and they had to be taken away from him. He stood the man up in the tractor but quickly lost interest.

Victoria said that what was noticeable in this setting was his ability to sit and remain on task. He was given several activities with a short break in between each activity.

James was observed by Victoria:

Cutting along a two-inch line of paper

Matching pictures

Putting together a Lego car

Putting together Mr Potato Head features following adult direction

Matching designs and colours

Selecting pictures of objects on request, for example, "Give me apple", "Give me hat" and so on

Matching correct colours to Care Bears (the names were provided by an adult)

At snack time James sat nicely. Opposite him was a girl aged six, but he took no notice of her. After lunch James played outside on the playground equipment. He seemed determined to find something he wasn't allowed. He finally found a shrub, broke a piece off and put it in his mouth. He had a minor tantrum when it was taken away from him, kicking out.

Victoria noted that James did not need to wear his

helmet during any of the work sessions. She said that because the environment James was taught in was highly structured and quiet he didn't seem to exhibit the difficult behaviours he had exhibited in the home and in the community. She noted that we had asked for further help in managing James' behaviour in the community, especially when we were out shopping.

Locomotive

James had shown an improvement since August. He was able to propel a tricycle forwards but without pedalling. This was an improvement from going backwards.

Manipulative Skills

Victoria noted that James demonstrated great dexterity, concentration and accuracy when he was given pieces of Lego to put together. He had also made progress here since August, from making marks on paper with a pen to making circular scribbles.

The assessment in August reflected that James was at least average with his visual skills. He was very strong in this area and was able to match abstract patterns very quickly and accurately.

Hearing and language skills (receptive language skills)

James immediately responded to "come" and "sit here". He could also hand over a familiar item when requested. He reluctantly put his hands on his head and shoulders when "Head, Shoulders, Knees and Toes" was sung. It was also reported by the therapists that he could clap his hands and wave bye-bye. Victoria did not observe James doing this during this assessment.

Speech and expressive language

James still had no meaningful language, although he was making progress by imitating sounds that the therapists made.

Self-care social

James' toilet-training had finally been achieved, which was a major improvement. He was out of nappies and, while he still wasn't requesting to go to the toilet, but he did indicate the need by pulling at his trousers. Using PECS at home was strongly advised.

Victoria had taken mine and Dale's view into consideration and had added it to her report as evidence. As James' parents we had seen a huge improvement in James' compliance and motivation in activities at home since he had started attending the ABA school. She also added that we were still experiencing difficulties while out in the community, but that we were expecting further help and support with this in the near future.

Victoria added conclusions and recommendations at the end of this subsequent assessment. She reported that within a matter of three months James' compliance and his ability to undertake activities that were not of his choosing had increased considerably. She added that James had great strength in terms of visual cognition and that this would help in developing his language skills and other aspects of learning. She went on to say that James would develop further because of his good visual perception skills, which would lead him to an object or word, and even to sentence use. These methods are used in both the PECS and ABA programmes.

Victoria advised that the ABA method should be continued with James and that intensive tuition should be maintained, which could later be extended within the community. A further assessment was to be carried out in three months' time after some integration within a mainstream school.

Victoria expressed her view that James was a severely autistic child and that autism was his main barrier to learning. He had made progress over this three-month period in many areas of his learning, particularly in imitation, compliance and the extension to keep on task. She noted that James' toilet-training had also been a huge success.

Victoria noted that James needed further intensive intervention with a strong emphasis on developing his communication, play and social interaction skills. She also stated that it would be of great benefit for speech and language therapists to work alongside the ABA therapists to devise an appropriate programme that would complement his ABA therapies.

It wasn't possible for us to use NHS speech therapists or OTs because as soon as we put James into the ABA school the local authority had pulled all of its services and support from us.

Psychological report (further addendum) 6th March, 2009

James had started attending a mainstream primary school one afternoon a week with the help of his ABA therapist Clare. The ABA school did this because the staff believed that gradually integrating James into a mainstream setting would give him additional benefits. Being exposed to a mainstream setting would allow him to model correct behaviours and could potentially even desensitise him to his peers and society, helping to make him ready for adult life.

It had been three months since Victoria Fone had seen or assessed James. For the following assessment, Victoria observed James at the mainstream school. This was James' seventh week at the school. The class James was in had a combined class of nursery and reception-aged children, comprising around 48 children in total.

The class teacher explained that James had initially stayed in her class for half an hour, and even though this was at a time when the class had been broken down into quiet groups, it was still difficult for him. She said that James had started to access toys when it was time to go, and he got distressed when they were removed from him. Despite this, they suggested increasing the time to an hour.

The teacher was happy to help James reach his target on his individual learning plan (IEP), but the head teacher had expressed concerns to Victoria that they did not feel they were meeting James needs. The school felt he wasn't interacting with other children and that large groups of children were distressing him. However, they were prepared to continue his sessions, regardless.

OBSERVATIONS

Victoria recorded that James was able to take off his coat and hang it up on the hook when shown a PECS picture showing the instruction with a verbal prompt. James was taken to a small bay area along with thirteen other children. James ran out of the area during a music session and Clare had to bring him back to his seat. James managed to sit for around a minute before he began to meddle with an instrument. At snack time, milk and tangerines were brought in and a mug of water was put in front of James. He used his PECS symbol to ask for his drink.

Victoria observed that James sat quietly during snack time for around four minutes before standing up. Clare said "sit here" (with a gesture) and he did. He sat for less than a minute before running out of the bay area. Clare brought him back and he continued with his snack for another three minutes.

He gestured that he needed the toilet by pulling at Clare towards his PECS board and selecting the toilet symbol. He managed to go to the toilet independently, although he needed verbal prompting to wash his hands. By this time all the other children had gone to play outside. James was shown the PECS symbol for putting his coat on and he managed this with little help.

Victoria reported that, while outside, James needed encouragement to hold hands with Clare. Other children wanted to join hands with Clare and James, but James ignored them. He used the PECS symbols again to request the toilet and he managed this independently.

James went inside to play with Clare in the home corner for a while. He briefly went into the cupboard, taking things out, dropping toy food on the floor and ripping labels off tins. James momentarily demonstrated some pretend play by putting a toy telephone to his ear for a few seconds.

Victoria added that she saw James briefly at our home, and that he was noticeably better at communicating his needs since she had seen him the previous December. She referred again to his spontaneous nature and recorded that he correctly used his PECS symbols to request the things he needed. She also pointed out that he appeared to be much calmer since her last visit.

She added that James could point to at least one hundred familiar objects by this point. While sitting quietly with his mother, he was able to select the correct object from a page. He was also vocalising more with obvious meaning by labelling pictures of Mama, Dada and Adam. He has been heard to say "no", and he asks for the door to be opened by saying "ope".

Conclusions and recommendations

Seeing James in a mainstream environment gave Victoria the opportunity to see how he reacted to other children and to note that the skills James had learnt at the ABA school were being generalised in other settings.

James sat down for a maximum of four minutes in one time and she said this seemed uncomfortable for him. He also made no attempt to interact with other children.

She said that James did exhibit very good use of his PECS book and that he had achieved this skill independently since she saw him December. She stated that being with James at the mainstream school was quite stressful for his ABA therapist because she had to be constantly vigilant of James. She said that alternative arrangements needed to be made, although she believed that the school activity groups were helping him to socialise.

Victoria expressed that James had made a considerable amount of progress since the previous September as a result of the intensive teaching methods of ABA therapy. She said that the teaching method was effective for James and that the help and support had been extremely beneficial to his parents.

PSYCHIATRIC REPORT

A psychiatrist called Dr Gloucester also completed a report on James when he was five years and two months old. It was done on 9th January, 2009. We travelled all the way to Canterbury in Kent, taking James with us. Dr Gloucester had been highly recommended to us. At the beginning of the assessment he gave us an overview of his experience and his career as a practitioner.

Dr Gloucester included evidence of progression through ABA therapy in his report. This was provided by us (his parents) and by various other professionals. Dr Gloucester observed that James was a highly complex young man and that he had severe impairments in terms of his empathy skills. He also reported that James did not have the ability to regulate his attention or arousal levels.

He noted the progress James had made since being on the ABA programme by showing that James could generalise new skills he had learnt and that his learning was retained after the reinforcers withdrew. He also recognised that James had severe sensory issues and that he would need to liaise with an OT. He noted that close school and home liaison was a must, with regular communication taking place between the two in order to share skills and ensure the consistency of programmes.

It was also noted that James had fragile academic self-esteem in addition to his autism, and that he had a very poor attention span and a severe language impairment. He advised that James required an intensive behavioural management plan to help with his lack of social and language skills, and that he also needed daily opportunities to reinforce and generalise his self-care and social interaction skills.

He added that children such as James run a twenty per cent risk of conduct difficulties and persistent depression in later childhood. He stated that, with a continuation of ABA therapy, James would further develop his potential from being preverbal and unmanageable to becoming a charming and inquisitive child who would be able to communicate more effectively with each year that passed.

Dr Gloucester also explained that the ABA school would provide the continuity and intensity that was essential if James' complex needs were to be met. He acknowledged that James' existing programmes were suiting him well and that he was demonstrating progress in all areas. He pointed out that James did have some way to go before he was able to internalise the skills he needed to survive without the intensive support of ABA therapy.

One thing that really stuck out to me from Dr Gloucester's report was something Dale and I had already seen. He noted that James was a good visual learner, that he was willing to please and could be motivated to learn, and that he was desperate to communicate. This marked him out as a good candidate for an ABA programme.

According to Dr Gloucester, literature-based evidence shows that early intervention with autistic children such as James means that, if they can develop useful communication and language, they will have up to a fifty per cent chance of a good level of social adjustment in later childhood and adulthood. This equates to semi-independent living at least. He also stated that premature extraction from the programme would have serious implications on public funding in the future. This would mean that when Dale and I became too old to look after James, more funds would be needed to fund a full-time residential care placement for him, which at the moment costs roughly two-hundred and fifty thousand pounds a year.

Dr Gloucester warned that James should carry on with his ABA programme with minimal disruptions at a time when he was making significant progress with his attention, empathy and socialisation skills, and in becoming more motivated to interact with adults and to develop language. Without ABA, Dr Gloucester said he would have a lower chance of achieving and of accessing the underlying ability that was masked by his autism and language impairment. He also stated that James would be at greater risk of developing serious challenging behaviour and mental health problems such as depression and anxiety disorders later on in life if he did not continue with ABA.

Typing all this out and reading the professional reports makes me feel so sad for James. This is why we shouldn't have had to fight for this. Anyone in their right mind could see that ABA therapy was the best way forward for James. Why would anyone want to disadvantage someone who is already at a disadvantage? It just doesn't seem right.

When I read other people's words describing James' autism it really hurts, even though we live with it every day. It's almost as though you become immune to the seriousness of it all. It's like living with back pain; you sort of get used to it. You get used to the high stress levels an autistic child gives you. It becomes a way of life. It's hard, but because you can't take a step back and see it all happening, you're blind to it in a way. It's only when you read it from someone else's point of view that you think, *God, it really is that bad.* This makes fighting for your child even more critical. The gloves are off and you give it all you've got because no one else will. We are all James has; the world doesn't give a shit.

***

We also had James assessed independently by a SALT and an OT. Again, an overview of James' complex needs was written up in great detail. Both made recommendations that James should have access to an OT for a thirty-minute block session twice a week and that a dietician would need to work closely with James regarding his food issues.

It was noted in the OT report that James had sensory processing disorder (SPD) as well as autism, which would be a disadvantage in the learning process. James' SALT report recommended that he should receive forty minutes to an hour of SALT per week and that the continued use of PECS symbols was a matter of urgency because he was experiencing communicative frustration. She also suggested that the SALT attended the monthly meetings at the ABA school so that the process would work more effectively for James.

All of these reports were sent to the Special Educational Needs and Disability Tribunal (SENDIST). We were happy with them. These people were at the top of their game and knew what they were talking about. We also handed in reports completed by the ABA school's educational psychologist, which was further evidence backing up the progress James had made.

CHAPTER EIGHT

The first-tier tribunal took place on 23rd March, 2009. There were three judges on the tribunal panel: Harry Lawson, William Thomas and David Johnson. On the appellant's side there was: me, Dale and our solicitor Adrian Slope. Our witnesses were James' ABA therapist Clare Flowers, consultant psychologist Alistair Henter and Victoria Fone.

The respondents in the case were the LEA, represented by Sharon Steely. Her witnesses were Wayne Floods and Sylvia Wool (the head teacher at Raven Top Primary School; a school for children with severe learning difficulties aged between two and eleven).

The evidence had been given to the judges via private assessments previous to the tribunal, including a summary of the rapid progress James had made in such a short space of time. James' extreme difficulties were discussed in depth during the tribunal because of the severity of his complex needs. It was strongly advised that he should be taught on a one-to-one basis within a low-stimulus environment.

Sylvia Wool did not think this was necessary, but the best she could offer was a small part of the classroom with a curtain pulled across. My witness, Victoria Fone, had been out to visit Raven Top Primary School and insisted that if James were to attend the school he would need individual support in a room by himself.

Wayne Floods agreed with Victoria on this point. However, he was booted under the table by Sharon Steely in a bid to shut him up. Adrian Slope, our solicitor, pointed out that even though Raven Top was an excellent school, it was not suitable for James, whose current programmes were eclectic. He pointed out that Raven Top did not have the facilities James required, and that James couldn't learn in groups because of his attention problems.

The original cost for James to attend Raven Top Primary school was £23,000 for thirty-five weeks of the year. The ABA school's costs were £43,000 for forty-nine weeks of the year. James would get specialist help at the ABA school with a team of four therapists, and he would be taught on a one-to-one basis. This included a monthly visit from the school's educational psychologist to assess his progress and to solve any issues that arose.

Dale and I had been attending this meeting once a month to see the progress James had made. Each and every time we attended, he had shown huge improvements and the new skills he had mastered were shown to us so we could maintain them at home.

James had not received any speech or occupational therapy during his time at the ABA school, but the school had managed to get him talking. Our local authority had pulled all support in those areas as soon as he started at the ABA school.

The problem we had then was that the local authority started to add all the costs on to the ABA schools. Costs such as SALT and OT took the total to £60,598, which was ridiculous really. James managed better without those therapies and he was making sufficient progress at a rapid rate. James had been at the Raven Top nursery, which was part of Ravens Top primary school, for two years. He had made no significant progress there at all despite those therapies he was supposedly getting there.

So we lost the tribunal based on cost issues, which was completely wrong. I wouldn't have needed the extra respite care during the school holidays, so they would have actually saved money on social care.

Also, our local authority had not factored in the cost of giving James his own teaching assistant. You can guarantee that cost would have been around £15,000, which would have brought their costs up to £38,000. And, if the ABA schooling hours were brought down to thirty-five weeks (pro rata) instead of forty-nine weeks, the ABA cost would have been down to £33,571, which would have been more cost-effective. The LEA would also have saved more money on transport and social care costs.

All the LEA needed to say at the tribunal was that they could meet James' needs and that they would have him placed in their school regardless of all the evidence we had provided. How unfair is that? Especially when they hadn't met his needs in the first place. They were caring for him rather than educating him. They had him sitting in nappies instead of teaching him self-care and independence. And we had to deal with violent temper tantrums instead of them giving him intensive speech therapy and teaching him to talk.

It's heartbreaking when you have no power or choice when it comes to getting what is needed for your severely disabled child. It's like living in a dictatorship, where they think that they're saving money when that couldn't be further from the truth.

Dale has the LEA's way of thinking summed up, and it goes a little bit like this: our local authority is a Labour-run council, and they seem to think that if they scrimp and penny-pinch now, by the time James is too big for us to handle and has to go into full-time residential care – costing the taxpayer £250,000 a year instead of the measly £43,000 we needed to keep him at home with his family for a year. They can look back and be proud that while they were in power they saved the government money and that when James goes into care, when he is older it won't be their problem; it will be some other political party that will have to deal with it.

As long as they feel satisfied with themselves, it's a job well done, even if it means crushing vulnerable families. We are the ones living with the heartache and the stress. Pat on the back for that. The way I see it is that if they spent more time giving children early intervention therapies such as ABA therapy it would result in less financial pressure on the system, in the long run.

They should use the money that they pay to all the high-flying judges who play God with people's lives and put that into educating children with special needs. Why put parents through expensive tribunal processes, which cost the LEA money (tax payer)? Legal professionals who are reading this will probably be seething at this statement. Well, I don't care. I feel angry and let down that you have made me lose faith in the system with your lies and promises.

***

James continued attending the ABA school while we appealed against the tribunal's decision. This took us from losing our tribunal on 23rd March, 2009, to being refused permission to appeal on 1st September, 2009, to being granted an oral hearing for the right to appeal in front of a judge in London at the Upper Tribunal chambers on 2nd November, 2009.

Back in June 2009 we had written to the council asking for the money James had been budgeted to go to Ravens Top Primary School. Between ourselves and the ABA school, we would have found the rest. I don't how we would have done so, but somehow we would have done it; we were so desperate. We had a reply back from the LEA saying that we should accept the tribunal's decisions, as they would do if it was the other way around. It's easy to say that when it's not your child and it's not your life that's affected.

They said that once a tribunal has reached a decision they could not go against it. Dale challenged them on this and said, "Okay, so what happens when you decide you can't cope with him at your school and you want to place him somewhere else? Does that mean he'll have to stay at the school you originally chose?" It was a ridiculous excuse really. Something could have been sorted out on a discretional basis.

We won the right to appeal at on 18th December, 2009, following a case that had been won previously that was very similar to ours. This was because the private assessment evidence we had collected had not been taken into consideration at the first-tier tribunal.

The appeal was adjourned for another two months. At this time I was heavily pregnant with Joel, our third child, and Dale had to go down to London on his own. Four months later we received a decision from the upper tribunal saying that it agreed with the verdict from the first tribunal. There was nothing more we could do; this was the end of the line.

CHAPTER NINE

James had received three years of ABA therapy by the time we finished going back and forth to tribunals. This was better than none at all, but he now had to go back to Ravens Top Primary School. Sylvia Wool was no longer head teacher at the school and the new head was called Patricia Lavender.

No sooner was James back there than his behaviour started to spiral out of control once again and he started to lose skills he had previously gained. I tried to get help from our local MP, but he gave us no hope either. He couldn't do anything because it had already been through the courts. Dale and I had meetings with the school and social services. We were going berserk because James' behaviour was deteriorating. In the meantime, the ABA school had closed down, so we literally had nowhere to turn and had to stop fighting for a full-time ABA programme because there was nowhere to send him.

We ended up having to put him in respite care twice a week just so we could get a break because things were becoming so difficult for us. This meant that he was classed as a 'looked-after child' (LAC) because the government had brought the respite hours down to seventy hours a year compared with the hundred and twenty it had been previously. I wouldn't have minded, but he probably didn't even hit the seventy-hour mark because we took him on lots of little holidays with us, which weren't factored in.

I remember going to see a doctor who did James' paediatric checks. He couldn't believe he was classed as an LAC just because he was in respite care from Saturday afternoon at 3pm until Sunday morning and then he went on a Monday night after school until school the following day. We did this because we needed a break, but because he was a very difficult child it wasn't like we had people queuing down the road to look after him.

Dale and I were so frustrated by the whole situation, especially when we saw all the hard work that had been done over the previous three years fall to pieces. We even had the guy who drove the school bus threatening to put James in a Houdini straitjacket. Dale and I were so angry because it had taken months and months to correct his behaviour in the car through intensive ABA therapy. We blatantly refused the idea of restraint. The way we saw it was that children like James need to regulate their own behaviour, otherwise they will always need adult intervention. We knew James was capable of this, and after the row we had with the driver and his boss we heard nothing more of it.

***

Meanwhile, we had meetings with social services about James concerning his behaviour due to him losing his ABA therapy. We also arranged a meeting with the head of children's services, who was in charge of social services and education, at our local council offices five months later. Two Conservative councillors attended the meeting with us and gave us representation, which I'm still very grateful for even to this day.

The outcome of that meeting was positive for us, as the head of children's services agreed a compromise. He agreed for an ABA consultant to come into Ravens Top Primary School for one day each term to train staff and to help set ABA programmes and behavioural strategies that worked with James. Social services reassessed our care package and agreed to let us use our funding to pay for a little ABA therapy at home. I also employed staff and paid them through direct payments. This made better sense and was a more beneficial use of time and money, rather than someone just supervising him around the house. It meant he was learning instead.

The new ABA consultant who started to work with James was called Michelle Fog, and funnily enough the recommendations and concerns that had been previously expressed by my independent witnesses in tribunal, started coming out of the mouth of this independent ABA consultant, who was employed by our local authority. One thing that springs to mind from what she said was that James needs to be taught in a classroom on his own for most lessons, in one-to-one sessions. She explained that classroom noise should be recorded and gradually turned up over a period of time so that he was able to get used to it.

There were lots of similarities between the recommendations she gave and the previous recommendations, which was very, very frustrating.

I must admit the school did try to compromise, but the amount of ABA therapy he was receiving wasn't enough to bring about the striking improvements the previous school had.

***

James was ten years old at this moment in time and he still couldn't read or write. James and Adam have since been diagnosed with attention hyperactivity disorder (ADHD). The medication has helped them both considerably, especially James, who is a lot calmer and more focused. The progress James made was very limited. I kept looking and looking for ABA schools in the north-west, but they all seemed to be down south. This was no good to us because they were too far away.

CHAPTER TEN

James had been back at the special needs LEA school for three years. He was receiving around twelve hours of ABA therapy at home each week and saw an ABA consultant once a term. The consultant was going into the school and training the staff in ABA therapy methods and techniques, as well as providing them with behavioural advice and ABA programmes.

Even though this was good to have, and we preferred this to no ABA at all, we could see that the progress James was making wasn't as great as the progress he had made when he was getting a full-time ABA programme at the ABA school.

Dale and I wanted the school's ABA consultant to work with our ABA staff at home because we wanted to strengthen the quality of James' ABA theory. We wanted to accelerate his progress because we saw that the progress he was making was very minimal. We were denied the option of using the school's ABA consultant, so I started to look into finding my own.

There is a well-known charity that specialises in ABA home programmes. It has a list of ABA therapists and consultants, who help parents, set up their own home programmes. The reason we didn't do this was that we couldn't afford to pay for a full-time ABA programme at home. It needed to be funded by the LEA, but there was no way we could afford to go back to a tribunal again.

The evidence we had provided the previous time had not been considered adequate, and we would have struggled even more to find evidence this time due to the lack of progress James had made. Peach put me in contact with its regional ABA consultant, who explained how she operated and the costs involved.

Dale and I already used direct payments to employ ABA staff, and seeing as we had been given a budget we didn't see a problem as long as we managed things carefully. There was no rule saying that we had to have the consultant every month. We could tailor the programme to suit our budget. Once again, we weren't asking for more money; we just needed permission to employ an ABA consultant, who could potentially improve James' quality of life. We were kept hanging on for months and months for a decision from the panel before being denied this proposal.

***

The other reason I had started getting really anxious about James and the ABA therapy was that I had been hanging on to one little thread, one little lifeline, and again this had disappeared out of my grasp. When James was at the ABA school, one of the families had moved to the UK from Ireland to get their daughter ABA therapy. The mother, Lorna Peppers, had read in an autism magazine about a celebrity whose daughter had received ABA therapy. It had worked wonders with her; in fact, it had worked so well she now attends a mainstream school.

This celebrity recognised that there was a huge shortage of ABA schools, especially up north, and understood the difficulties children faced in being able to access an ABA programme. ABA had made a life-changing difference for his daughter and he wanted to help other families who were in the same predicament. He had started raising money for the Hearts and Minds Challenge to help it set up an ABA school in Manchester. He was still raising funds five years later.

The school underwent a lengthy application process, and it has since come to my attention that it won't exclusively be offering ABA therapy, even though ABA can be provided. It will provide educational programmes tailored to each child's needs. The other problem that came to light was that the school only caters for children aged three to eleven.

When I found this out I was absolutely mortified, because the new school was all I had been hanging on to. After the previous three years of tribunals, this was the only hope in my mind of getting James a full-time ABA programme. Having lost the tribunal and finding out that the ABA school was closing down there was no point in continuing to fight the LEA because there was no ABA school to send him to. I had been holding all my fight for this new school and suddenly it was gone.

I phoned the charity's founder Ian McGrath, who I had had contact with previously regarding James' case, and I told him I felt like giving up. I couldn't believe how far away we were from getting James' needs met once again. It was like another heavy blow. I felt fear and panic because there seemed to be no hope for my son. It made me feel as though I might as well hand him over there and then because what's the point in prolonging the agony? We knew we couldn't and wouldn't ever be able to have a normal life if we couldn't get our son the right help. We stood no chance.

I was gutted, and with the pain I felt in my gut and throat I felt as though I had been floored. Dale and I are very resilient people. For those of you that know us, we put up with high stress levels and we are used to it. We make a good team and we will never give up, but when I heard this I was left feeling hopeless. To keep having every door slammed in your face when all you want to do is provide your son with what he should be entitled to makes you feel like screaming and ripping the walls down.

Ian McGrath said he would come to our house to visit us to see what he could do to help us and James. He did this and he told us he would put us in contact with a lady called Louise Gorman. He said she could advocate for us and help us get the correct support for James. She was one of the charity's educational advocates and had years of experience in the special educational needs field.

The argument was originally about the direct payment money, which we wanted to use to get James an ABA consultant. The charity couldn't understand why we were being denied this help. We explained the whole story and Louise could see straightaway that there were a lot of discrepancies, especially concerning James' special educational statement. The first thing I needed to do, she said, was photocopy all of James' recent annual reviews, ABA reports and his special educational statement.

***

While all this was happening behind the scenes, James' behaviour was starting to become a real nightmare. His latest fixation was unlit candles, and in the end we had to stop him having them because it was getting to the point where he was occasionally eating the wax. And if he spotted them in someone else's house he wanted them. So we decided he wasn't allowed them at all.

Things started coming to a head when I took James and Joel to get some shopping from Sainsbury's and bumped into my friend Kim. Joel had just turned three at the time, so in essence it was like I was dealing with two children of a similar age. James had spotted some candles, and no matter what distraction techniques I used nothing worked.

Kim could see that he was getting highly stressed and that he kept bolting into the aisle where the packs of tapered candles were stored. I kept pulling him away and trying to get him to stand still while I attempted to put my shopping through the self-service till. Kim and I more or less took it in turns to put the shopping through as we watched Joel and chased after a screaming James. He was hell-bent on running down the shopping aisle, screaming and shouting, while trying to rip open the packets of candles.

The whole supermarket seemed to come to a standstill. Onlookers were staring, wondering what the hell was going on with their open-mouthed expressions. I couldn't really have given a crap! I had made a decision and I needed to stick to it. If I had given in there and then by buying the candles it would have set a precedent for future situations. The following week's tantrum would only have had to raise the bar slightly and *bang*, that's where out-of-control behaviour starts.

James' face was getting redder and redder as he was running around and we both had bubble coats on. We were wrestling around at the till, and he kept dropping to the floor for no reason. I got too hot and tired to deal with him, as I had Joel and the shopping to deal with. I asked Kim to get the shop's security guard to help me get him back to the car.

James' rage did not calm down once he was back in the car. He tried to kick the car windows in and also tried to slap Joel. I was stuck in Sainsbury's car park for three quarters of an hour, unable to drive anywhere. If I had driven anywhere he would have attacked me, and there was a high risk that I would have crashed the car.

I can tell you now that my blood was boiling with all this, "No, you can't have this help and you can't have that help". It was absolutely ridiculous. I couldn't even go to the shops without it being a majorly stressful event, not to mention the effect these situations were having on my other children. All this incident did was add to my anger even more.

***

I got on the phone to my family support worker and said that I was going to drop James off at Beatrix House, where he went for overnight respite care, if they couldn't help me convince the LEA to give us what we needed in order to get through life. All this drama was like a prison sentence. The family support worker rang me back within half an hour and said the only thing they would offer me was a one-off consultation with an ABA consultant. All I can say was that this was absolutely laughable!

Having a consultant goes hand in hand with ABA therapy, and it needs to be ongoing. The excuse I got from my family support worker was that she was finding it difficult to get the head of social services, Deirdre Lytton, who was her boss, to ring her back. She said she would ask her again to see if she would change her decision. I got a call back to say that Deirdre wouldn't budge. We could have a one-off consultation and that was it.

Dale became as frustrated as me. He wanted to speak to Deirdre to explain our situation and the benefits of having an ABA consultant. We really couldn't understand what the problem was. All we wanted to do was use our direct payment package to fund this; we weren't asking for more money.

Dale had phoned social services four times a day for two weeks. He was constantly told that Deirdre was on the other line and would phone him back. Or that Deirdre was in a meeting or out of the office and she would ring him back. After two weeks there was still no call back. There was no acknowledgement and Dale and I were getting more and more annoyed because it was unprofessional and we were really desperately struggling with James. The time Dale had to take out of his working day to constantly phone and then constantly be fobbed off was so frustrating. We felt like we were banging our heads against a brick wall.

***

Dale and I took James, Adam and Joel away to Wales for a short holiday. This was just after Christmas and James' behaviour was very up and down. The slightest thing would spark him off. We had bought Adam a game for Christmas called *Pop to the Shops*. If we said "shops" it would spark off a tantrum. The persistent shouting and screaming for shops was getting too much, so we had to code the game and call it PTS.

Mealtimes were also a nightmare. As soon as we started to cook he started having a meltdown. He would shout "no, no" and when we gave him his meal he would scream more, digging his plate into his lap. On one occasion he asked for chips and was becoming distressed, screaming because he had to wait for them to be cooked. Then, when they were cooked, he didn't want them. The whole situation was so stressful and it wasn't nice for our other two children to witness it.

One day we decided to go out walking on the beach.

We must have been out for around three hours, and we popped into a cafe that sold little knick-knacks. I bought James a glass ball pendant on a string. He loves this kind of thing and I thought it would calm him down and give him something to focus on. It did until we decided to go back to the caravan and drive to the shops in the town centre to get a couple of things.

While we were in the shop, James spotted a chocolate rabbit. For some reason he has a fascination with them, and has had for several years. He loves the red ribbon and the bell around the neck. If he has one he won't eat the rabbit straightaway, he will walk around holding it for a few hours like some kind of trophy.

Dale and I decided we didn't want to buy James a chocolate rabbit because the food issue was getting worse and letting him fill up on chocolate would only add to the behaviour. James is usually very good at accepting when we say no. We haven't gone through life giving in to him and pandering to his autism because we are frightened of a meltdown. I seriously believe that if we hadn't parented him the way we have done he would be a hundred times worse than he is now.

This time James did not accept no, and he started screaming and shouting. Dale left the shop with him and I was left with Adam and Joel as I paid for the shopping. When I started walking up the high street with the two boys and the shopping, I could see Dale and James further on in the distance. They were heading towards the car and James was still having a tantrum. It had escalated, so James was hitting Dale and dropping to the floor. Onlookers stood watching in disbelief.

The boys and I were halfway to the car when we saw Dale drive past with a screaming James in the back. He was totally out of control. I knew Dale was heading back to the shop we had been in, so we made our way back there. I got to the car park and put the lads and the shopping in the car. James was going absolutely ballistic.

Dale was really upset and highly stressed because on the way back to the car park James had unclipped his seatbelt and was hitting Dale in the head while he was driving. James had been holding the crystal pendant and had thrown it in temper across the busy main road, missing a parked car and a child by just a foot on the opposite side of the road.

James was at the point of no return and had started to hit Adam and Joel. I decided to get him out of the car to calm him down and keep him from hurting anyone else. He was going wild, hitting and squeezing me. Meanwhile, Dale decided to phone Beatrix House to explain the situation. James was due in that night for respite care but I had phoned the night before to cancel as we had decided to take him away.

Linda, who was one of the carers at Beatrix House, told Dale he could bring James in anyway because they had not filled his place. Dale was overwhelmed by the whole situation. The ABA techniques we had used over the years had no effect. Nothing seemed to work and he was becoming a danger to himself and others. We had no control at all.

This behaviour had been building for a few months. We were getting no support and social services wouldn't return our calls. Dale told Beatrix House he was going to drop him off and that he would not be picking him up the day after. We had had enough and we couldn't cope, especially with the lack of support. Dale then drove James to Beatrix House. It was a five-hour round trip.

We both felt absolutely devastated that things had got this bad. We were just trying to do the best for our children. We were trying our best to give them a lovely life with happy memories, but it was such a struggle to achieve this. All we wanted was to be good parents and to enjoy our family life. We were screaming out for help and we weren't getting it. The whole situation left us feeling numb and we really felt as though we had no choice but to leave him at Beatrix House. It may seem extreme, but no one would listen and no one would help us. We felt burnt out by it all.

The next day another staff member from Beatrix House, Lorraine, phoned us. She explained that if we didn't pick James up it would be classed as abandonment and a senior social services officer would ring us in the afternoon. This never happened. James' next visit to Beatrix House was on the Monday night, so the only night he stayed when he shouldn't have was the Sunday.

***

By Monday there had still been no phone call from social services. The only person who rang was a member of staff called Paul from Beatrix house. He said James was okay for that night as he was booked in for respite anyway. He told me James was fine, even though we had already phoned previously to see how he had been. They said that he had been a little quiet, but on the whole he had been fine. He said James would be dropped home by the school bus on the Tuesday night as usual. I told him this was not going to happen and that I wanted Deirdre to contact us as we needed more help and support.

Meanwhile, I had tried getting in touch with various local councillors to try and get some support from them. That night we received an email from Deirdre stating that we were going to be charged under section 47 of the Children Act 1989 for the abandonment, and the emotional abuse and neglect of James. I couldn't believe it! All we needed was more help and support. We felt like we had been pushed into a corner and that we had no choice.

The really annoying thing is that we had fought tooth and nail to get James the right help and support, only to be denied it by the local authorities. What gives them the right to have this power over our lives? It was like a prison sentence of misery. Why did our family have to struggle and live a life of unhappiness and sadness at the expense of the local authorities, who were cheating us and our son out of the education and support he truly deserved? It's heartbreaking and it saddens me to the core that we had been put in this position in the first place. We love our children so much; anyone who knows us will tell you this. I felt physically sick with worry and stress.

Deirdre could not attend the meeting at our house on the Tuesday afternoon, but she sent round a new social worker along with a senior member of staff from social services. They wanted us to sign paperwork work there and then under section 47 for putting him into voluntary foster care. They told us that if we let James go he might end up with a family far away. This wasn't what we wanted, and they were pushing us to sign there and then. We would obviously never have done this and we told them we would have James back that night. We had really missed him and I was so relieved to get him back.

***

A meeting was set up with Deirdre to discuss the issues we were having with James. Louise Gorman came with us to represent us. Louise brought up the fact that James' special educational needs statement did not match up. She explained that with the therapies and support he was missing out on it was no wonder James was getting into trouble and we were struggling, because the whole thing wasn't worth the paper it was written on.

One of the other major concerns raised in the meeting was that Beatrix House was closing for three months for a full refurbishment. The problem with this was that they weren't providing like-for-like provision. They were providing day care instead, which wouldn't provide us with the support we needed.

The Family Link service was discussed, but we

were always against this idea because James cannot speak, and even though the families are police checked you can never be too sure who else goes in and out of someone's home. Then there were the safety concerns. What if someone accidentally left the front door open? James has no road sense, so this was another major worry. In the end we decided that one of my ABA therapists would provide James with respite care, so this worked out well for us.

***

I was really concerned about James' aggression levels. He was under a psychiatrist called Dr Hughes for his ADHD, so I contacted her after the incident in Wales and spoke to her about my concerns. I wondered if she might be able to prescribe James something that would calm his anxiety levels.

She suggested that I make an appointment with her, so I agreed and she offered us one right away. While we were in the waiting room, James started to become very stressed. He was shouting and whinging. Even when we were in Dr Hughes' room he was carrying on. I told her all about James' aggression and frequent meltdowns, asking her whether it was possible to put him on beta-blockers or something as it was pretty obvious he was suffering from very high anxiety levels.

Dr Hughes said they sometimes offer a drug called Risperidone to calm aggression, but due to the side-effects she was very reluctant to prescribe it to a child like James. She explained that children like James have sensitive brains, and that if he were to have an adverse side-effect he could be left with permanent damage, including ticks or muscle spasms.

I asked again about prescribing James beta-blockers, but she said she couldn't prescribe them long term and that this wouldn't be the correct solution for James. She advised me that the best thing to do was up the ADHD medication instead. If that didn't work we would look at Risperidone.

I remember driving to the doctor's surgery to put James' prescription in and feeling desperate. If this didn't work, what then? I felt tired, hopeless, powerless and generally pissed off. We had tried other remedies such as aromatherapy oils and Rescue Remedy, but nothing seemed to work. Surprisingly, James' drug increase worked and his anxiety levels did calm down. I can tell you now, that was a massive relief.

We were eagerly awaiting James' annual review at that school so that we could find out what changes were needed and to ask about the services he should have been receiving. While this was going on, the school had agreed to send out their ABA consultant to do some work with James and to liaise with James' home-based ABA team, so things were starting to come together.

Michelle Fogg was due to visit James at home on 24th February, 2014, and we were really pleased about this because we wanted to strengthen James' ABA treatment and hopefully start to see faster progress.

***

The school was due to break up for half-term on Friday 14th February. James had his ABA therapy on the Thursday night as usual and later on that night, he said "Sick!"

That night I bathed James and his brothers and put them to bed. By 10.15pm James started to be sick, and I was in and out of his room most of the night. He didn't fall asleep until 8am on the Friday morning. Dale and I thought this was unusual going by past experience. Whenever James had had a bug before he would never have stayed up all night being sick. At some point he would have fallen asleep.

I remember saying to Dale that I had a feeling James had swallowed something and Dale agreed, seeing as James had been awake all night. I phoned our GP and the receptionist said she would get a doctor to ring me back. Our surgery offers a telephone consultation with a doctor and then the doctor decides whether or not you need an appointment.

I explained to Dr Amber that James was severely

autistic and that he couldn't express himself properly, and that he also suffers with pica disorder; an appetite for non-nutritive substances. I expressed my concerns that he had been up all night vomiting and that if it had been a bug he would have fallen asleep.

Dr Amber assured me that if James had swallowed something he definitely wouldn't be being sick. He told me to keep an eye on him and advised that if he wasn't any better within a couple of days I should bring him to the surgery and he would have a look at him.

I phoned his school and spoke to the receptionist, explaining that James had been being sick all night and would not be coming in. I also asked her if there had been any sickness bugs going around. She said that there had, but only among the younger kids.

James slept most of Friday and he had stopped vomiting and by Saturday he had eaten some toast and had a cup of tea. But I was left with a niggling feeling that something wasn't quite right with him. I had noticed that he was holding his breath every now and again and that he was walking with a funny gait.

I decided to take him to our local accident and emergency department. On arrival, I explained what was going on with James and that he was also severely autistic so he wasn't good at waiting. We saw a triage nurse and I explained the whole scenario again. I told the nurse my thoughts about him having swallowed something.

They arranged for James to have an X-ray done to see if they could find any foreign objects in his body, but nothing showed up. A nurse examined James, did some observations and then had a feel of his tummy. As soon as she did this he nearly jumped through the roof. It was clear that he was really in pain.

She said she was going to take some bloods and I warned her that she might have a fight on her hands because when he had had blood tests done in the past I had literally had to pin him down. To my surprise he just let them do it. He must have felt really ill. James and I waited in the small side room for an hour until the nurse came back with the results.

They said that all the blood tests had come back normal apart from one. This was the one that showed if any infection was present, but it was only showing a slight abnormality. She said this could happen sometimes if a child has appendicitis. More bloods are usually affected in the case of appendicitis, but it's not too unusual for just one to be affected.

James and I were transferred upstairs to an observation ward and a surgeon came round to speak to me. He said he was going to treat James for suspected appendicitis. I told the surgeon that I didn't think this was the case. I knew the X-ray hadn't shown anything up, but that didn't mean there wasn't anything in there. I mentioned again that James was known for swallowing threads and other items that might not necessarily show up on an X-ray.

I asked if James could have a scan done because I

was adamant that he was more likely to have ingested something inedible rather than it being appendicitis. This was all a gut feeling; an instinct I have learnt to trust thorough past experience. The surgeon said that there wasn't anyone to do the scan because it was a Saturday night and they had no out-of-hours scanner.

I was getting really stressed because the doctor's professionalism was clashing with my experience of being James' parent. I asked them to transfer him to the children's hospital because they had an out-of-hours scanner there and I didn't want to put my child's life at risk because of a lack of medical resources. They said that I could discharge James if wanted to, but I would then have to start the process all over again, starting right back at the accident and emergency department.

CHAPTER ELEVEN

James was given a scan the following day, and he was very stressed by the situation. We couldn't work out whether this was because he was in pain and didn't want anyone touching his tummy, or if it was because he had taken an instant dislike to the cold, wet gel they use for the scan procedure.

When you are autistic like James, things that don't feel too bad to us feel horrendous to them. He wouldn't keep still; he was continually wriggling and screaming. The sonographer said there appeared to be a slight calcification around the appendix area and that this can be a classic sign of appendicitis.

James was due to go into surgery that night for his appendix to be removed, but an emergency case came in so it was put off until the following day. In the morning the team of surgeons that would be operating on James came round to see us and explained the whole procedure.

When it was time for James to be collected for surgery I went down to the anaesthetic room. It's horrible seeing your child in this situation, but what are you meant to do? Needs must and it was important to get him better. The operation was expected to take an hour, but they told me it sometimes took longer, so we were warned not to worry if this was the case.

James had been in the operating theatre for around half an hour when Dale and I were called down to see the surgeon who was carrying out the operation. We were informed on the way down that when an appendix operation is carried out they have to pull the bowel out first to get to the appendix. When they pulled the bowel out they had found the tip of a yellow piece of plastic that had perforated his bowel. According to the surgeon, there was also something else in there.

He asked if we had any idea what it was and he wasn't very impressed to say the least. We didn't know what it was, and we didn't know when the incident was likely to have happened. We had to give permission for the surgeon to remove the items because they only had our legal consent to remove his appendix. They removed the items, repaired his bowel and left his appendix untouched as there was nothing wrong with it.

One of the surgery team who worked in anaesthetics told us that if we had not kept on at them about James' unusually placid and calm behaviour they would have sent him home and his bowel would have died. James would not only have had to contend with his severe autism, which is seriously deliberating, he would also have had a colostomy bag for the rest of his life. All this proves once again that, as parents, we know our son better than anyone else. We don't need a doctor's degree or to be qualified up to the eyeballs. We have life experience as well as common sense, and that's the real formula.

I went down to recovery to collect James, and when I saw the condition he was in I was shocked and angry, especially when I saw the removed items which were waved about in front of me in a pathology bag. There were two items: a four-inch yellow rubber worm; and a three-inch orange rubber worm. I knew that he hadn't swallowed them at home.

James was very distressed. He was moaning and crying and trying to get off the bed. His eyes were glazed and I felt so sorry for him. I couldn't help but cry, because even though he was ten years old this situation proved to me that he's really only a baby. It reminded me why we always have to fight so hard for him; he is so vulnerable.

One of the surgeons from the operating team said that as soon as he had come around from the anaesthetic, James had ripped the tube out of his mouth. They couldn't believe how quick he was. I sat on the bed and cuddled James, and I ended up explaining the whole story to the surgeons. They were shocked. They couldn't understand why this child couldn't have a therapy that worked so well for him.

They wheeled James back up to the ward with me alongside, and Dale was there waiting. I showed him the pathology bag with the items James had swallowed in it. Dale was also shocked.

***

Although it was half-term, I knew there would be someone on the site at the school. I told Dale I was going to go in to see if I could see any worms in his classroom. I also phoned Louise Gorman to tell her what had happened to James and explained that I was going to the school. When I got there the only two people that were in, were the school secretary and the head teacher's PA.

I explained that James was under investigation at Tameside Hospital and that I needed have a look around James' classroom to see what he had access to; as we thought he might have swallowed something. When I went into the classroom the rubber worms were displayed on the table along with PECS symbols, which displayed images of size. I asked if I could take a photo of them and the head teacher's PA said that was okay. She explained that his class teacher had only put them out on the Friday, which was James' first day of absence.

I left shortly after this and phoned Louise again, explaining my findings in the classroom. Louise had read all the reports about James and his special educational needs statement, so she was well-informed. James had to have one-to-one supervision at all times and this was clearly written in his statement. She immediately agreed that he had not been getting one-to-one in the classroom and that the school was well aware that James has pica. She contacted a solicitor on my behalf so that there would be one less thing for me to sort out.

***

Back at the hospital, James was sleeping and Dale was sitting by his side waiting for me to return. He couldn't believe I had managed to get into the classroom, let alone that I had proof. I was really annoyed, and Dale and I agreed that he couldn't go back to that school. Enough was enough. His life had been put at risk and this should not have happened.

James had a dressing over the wound where the incision was and he was given intravenous antibiotics and Oramorph, a children's version of morphine. They also gave him paracetamol but refused to give him ibuprofen because his stomach was empty. He wasn't allowed to eat until he had either broken wind or had a bowel movement, because after a major operation like this the bowel goes to sleep and stops working. The last thing they wanted was to cause any further trauma to his bowel.

Everything had to be done very slowly. At first I had to give him small sips of juice from a syringe and then they said they would send a dietician around to discuss what I could feed James on. The dietician said James had to go on a low-fibre diet, which is really difficult when you have a child as fussy as James. I also asked her if she dealt with children with food aversions who suffered with pica. I was shocked and angry when she told me this was part of a speech therapist's job. The whole thing is farcical, as that was something else James wasn't receiving.

James' pica was no secret to anyone. Even Beatrix House knew about it as a member of staff there had once had to do the Heimlich manoeuvre on him because he had swallowed a rubber glove. I was close to tears again with anger that no one had offered us the support we needed with this. The whole system is a disgrace!

***

I found it quite difficult at first in hospital when James wasn't allowed to eat a lot, because he was trying to swallow things like staples from the display boards and pasta from the children's artwork on the walls, not to mention the Play-Doh in the children's playroom.

One thing I discovered during our stay in hospital was that he loved painting. He can't paint anything in particular, but he loves mixing all the colours together and he spends a considerable amount of time doing it. This is a first for James because his attention span is very poor. The amazing thing is, when they are dry you can see things in his paintings: faces, animals and so on.

After a week in hospital the nursing staff were happy to let James go home. They were happy with the way his wound was healing and he was more or less pain-free. They also said that he would be better settled at home after seeing him have a huge meltdown because the food they were serving up wasn't to his liking.

Back at home, James kept asking me to paint so I went out and bought him acrylic paints, canvases, glitter gel pens and other bits and pieces. He got to a point where he was asking to paint every day, so I thought it would be a nice idea to give him his own Facebook page. I called it James' autism paint therapy. I thought it would be nice and a bit of fun to share his newfound hobby.

James stayed in my full-time care while he made a full recovery. I stopped him going to Beatrix House because the week before the accident James had swallowed two rubber carrots and his dad had found them in the toilet. Both the school and the respite facility denied that this was them, but these were the only two settings he had been in and the carrots were definitely not from home.

After the operation I felt like I couldn't trust anyone. It was difficult caring for him all day and night, as well as having a three-year-old who only attended nursery in the afternoons. Being the cheeky monkey he is, Joel thinks it's hilarious to copy everything James does, so it was like double the work. Adam was eight by this point and has

ADHD and an oppositional defiant disorder, so things can be difficult and tiring. Having to battle with professionals all the time made it worse. This is why we have Louise advocating for us. She and the hearts and minds challenge charity have been an absolute godsend!

James' annual review was due and Louise was appalled to find that when the school sent out the invitation they hadn't done it properly. We didn't know which professionals would be attending the review and we certainly didn't have the necessary reports from all the professionals involved in James' care.

A letter had to be drafted with Louise's help and sent off to the school saying that the review had to be put off until a further date so that we could have all the relevant information. In the meantime, the school and Beatrix House kept phoning to ask how James was and when he was likely to be back. I had to keep telling them he was still recovering because I no longer trusted either setting. If I sent him back to school that would suggest that everything was ok, but it wasn't. These settings were putting my child at risk and that was something I could not let happen again.

***

We recently found another school that teaches ABA therapy. It isn't an ABA school, but it does have an ABA unit attached to it. It teaches children with autism and severe learning difficulties from the age of three to nineteen.

I was really impressed when Dale and I looked around it because it also has a college setting with a hair salon, woodwork shop, kitchen and a place outside for growing vegetables. I liked this because I thought this was how it should be. Autistic children need normality and life skills. The other thing I thought was good was that there was no transition from primary to secondary school, or secondary school to college, because it's all based at the same site.

The annual review meeting was on 24th March, 2014. All the correct reports had been sent out prior to the meeting this time, and all the professionals involved in James' care attended the meeting. The attendees were: me, Dale, Louise Gorman, Patricia

Lavender, Joanne Mooney, Wayne Floods, James' classroom teacher Catrina Flair and social worker Kenzi Smith.

We started to go through James' educational statement, reading out that James needed SALT once a week, and that the speech therapist needed to work closely with us to make sure we all got the correct support. This had never happened. We had never seen the speech therapist that was at the meeting before. Ongoing support from occupational therapy was another service James had not received.

He was also supposed to have a teaching assistant giving him full one-to-one support for thirty-two-and-a-half hours a week. He never got this either, if the swallowing incident is anything to go by. I had sent Patricia Lavender an email informing her about the swallowing incident and she had replied saying that they were trying to give him more independence in the classroom. Ongoing physiotherapy was another service that had been written into James' statement that he wasn't receiving.

Everyone added their views about their involvement with James apart from Kenzi Smith. I really don't know why she bothered coming. She doesn't know us very well so she wasn't really able to contribute.

I made it quite clear in the meeting that I was absolutely disgusted and fuming. I explained that our local authority had fought us in court, which had stopped our son from receiving the help and support he needed. I wanted Kenzi to see the other side of the story. On top of that there was the financial impact it had had on us.

I explained that the LEA had also added therapy costs for out-of-house services to the ABA school fees, making their school of choice look cheaper and more appealing to the judges so that it appeared favourable in terms of public expenditure. But as a result, James had not been getting the help he needed.

This had made his behaviour much more difficult, so we had needed more respite care. I explained that he only stayed overnight twice a week, but because the government had brought the hours down to seventy hours a year and that it used to be one hundred and twenty hours a year instead, James then had been classed as a LAC, which was voluntary (our choice!). I also said that James probably went less than that because we took him on a lot of holidays, and that the annoying thing was that if James had received the right help and support we probably wouldn't have needed the respite in the first place.

It's really annoying to have a social worker who doesn't even have children sitting there judging you instead of going out of her way to make a difference and do everything she can to help and support you. I'm sick of being judged by people who have no idea what it's like to walk in my shoes. I really wish they had a week to see and feel what it's like, especially to feel what it's like to be judged. There really is no worse feeling.

The education officer tried to skip past part five of the statement, which related to James' school placement. We told them we wanted James to go to a different school, which was out of our borough. Joanne Mooney explained that this decision would have to go to a panel.

The problem with this sort of thing is that everything takes such a long time. Panel meetings take place once a month and then there are school holidays, so you feel like you're hanging on for a lifetime. All I wanted to do was get my son into this new school, get him a full-time ABA programme and get on with our lives without all this stress and worry.

***

In the meantime, I phoned social services to speak to Rachel Hornet. Who was dealing with my direct payment package for James' social care. She is lovely, down-to-earth and very approachable. However, I ended up with Kenzi at the other end of the line saying that Rachel was on another line and asking if she could help instead. I explained that since James would no longer be attending Beatrix House because I no longer trusted anyone to look after my son, I wanted him to be taken off the LAC register. The response I got was patronising and it got my back up. She said: "I don't think it quite works like that, Sarah."

I thought to myself, *Do you know what, I'm not getting into a row with someone who doesn't know what they're talking about.*

"Just get Rachel to phone me back," I said.

Kenzi replied, "I can ask her, Sarah."

My response was, "Oh right, are we going to have to phone up four times a day for two weeks just to get a response, like last time?"

Fortunately, Rachel phoned back straightaway and I explained that I didn't trust anyone with James. She understood exactly what I meant. Sure enough, I received a letter saying that James was no longer a looked-after child.

I would rather struggle with no help than be looked down on and judged by people who have no idea. I've had to protect my child from the local authorities, which sounds crazy when they're meant to be the good guys. Hardly! Families like us are just a number and a sum of money to them. It's so sad when all you want to do is get by in life and be happy and know that your children are happy.

They didn't want to give James the help because he was born like that. If they had just looked at the bigger picture and given him the therapy he needed it could have made such a difference to him. We already have proof that it works.

The LEA agreed for James to go to the new provided that they had a place for him. I was just hanging on for the new school to get back to me. They had his statement and I was praying to God every day that James would get a place. I even visualised him in the uniform. I wanted to shut this book at the end of our fight for education, happy in the knowledge that my child was getting what he needs, and that we could look forward to the future.

James was accepted into the new School in September 2014 and also won the right to a full-time ABA therapy programme. Words cannot express how thrilled we are! We are so excited and cannot wait to see the progress James is going to make. He had already made a considerable amount of progress with his speech in my full-time care, and I hadn't even been home-schooling him. We knew that the possibilities for him were endless now that he was in the correct educational setting.

EPILOGUE

Having a child with autistic spectrum disorder has been very challenging for me. I have found James' condition very difficult to deal with. It has been very stressful dealing with temper tantrums, difficult behaviours and the constant worry about his future.

On a positive note, having a child like James has helped me grow as a person. He has taught me a lot about life, other people and myself. Without James I would never have known that I was capable of writing this book. He has taught me that self-worth comes from within and that we should not let our self-worth be measured by society's expectations.

He has helped me realise that we would all do far better if we did what we loved, particularly if we were given more encouragement to pursue these activities from a young age. I believe that we all possess some sort of gift, but that some people never get a chance to unwrap theirs.

James has taught me a lot of important lessons in

life. He has been one of my great teachers, that's for sure. I remember a time when he was small and all he used to do was stim. He still stims, but he has also found other interests. He likes to paint, he likes to help me cook and he can swim underwater as if he were amphibious. These are interests he derives pleasure from.

He is eleven now and he still can't read and write. But I have faith that this will happen and I will always believe in him. I never thought he would talk but he did, and I guess what I'm trying to say is, never give up! I think we are sent lessons in life for spiritual growth, really. That's how I have decided to look at it and I don't care whether or not we fit in with other people's expectations. The most important thing is love and happiness.

The way I see it is that James has found things that he enjoys doing. You can't make him fit into any of the 'normal' boxes, so I notice his interests and help him turn them into strengths. One day he will become a master of them. These interests are life skills and gifts. They can never be taken away.

Now that James is receiving the correct educational provision with full-time ABA therapy I feel confident that he will flourish. My mind is finally at peace. The most exciting thing for us now is watching him grow and progress.

I wanted to give people out there some hope. If you keep on fighting, you will succeed in the end. For those who are struggling on the autism journey, please never lose faith in yourself or your children. Never give up the fight for them. It isn't easy, but only you can do it.

Useful Contacts

Hearts and Minds Challenge Charity

6 Dunollie Road

Sale

Manchester

M33 2PD

07540 558788

Ian@heartsandmindchallenge.org

https://www.facebook.com/HeartsAndMindsUK

ESPA Research

The Robert Luff Laboratory

Unit 133i

North East Business & innovation Centre

(BIC)

Sunderland Enterprise Park

Wearfield, Sunderland

SR5 2TA

Telephone from the UK

0191 549 9300

Telephone from outside the UK

00 44 191 549 9300

Facebook pages

James'autism paint therapy

Jimmy, Me and Autism Memoir

jimmymeandautism@gmail.com

Printed in Great Britain
by Amazon.co.uk, Ltd.,
Marston Gate.